Tea *of* Life

Tea *of* Life

Stories from the
GOODRICKE GARDENS

SATHYA SARAN
Photos by Supriya Kantak

Harper
Collins

First published in hardback in India by
HarperCollins *Publishers* in 2021
A-75, Sector 57, Noida, Uttar Pradesh 201301, India
www.harpercollins.co.in

2 4 6 8 10 9 7 5 3 1

P-ISBN: 978-93-5422-273-3

Typeset in 13/16 Bell MT by Meena Rajasekaran

Printed and bound at
Thomson Press (India) Ltd.

Dedicated to everyone living in the tea gardens, who makes enjoying a fine cup of tea possible.

चाय!

होंटों से जब चूम के देखोगे, तब जानोगे
अच्छी चाय क्या होती है

एक पहाड़ी धूप का रँग
दूजे भाप से उड़ती ख़ूश्बू
बिना तक्कलुफ़ नाक को छू के
अपने आप तारूफ़ करवाती है अपना

चाय का भी तो अपना एक मिज़ाज होता है
आग पसन्द नहीं है उसको
उबला उबला पानी डालो___
बन्द कैटल में बैठ के उसमें घुल जाती है
रँग आ जाता है चेहरे पर

तीन तीन सिंगार हैं उसके...
दूध का छूआँ, चुट्की भर सिंदूर के जैसा
या एक 'त्राशा' निम्बू का, मुस्कान के जितना
वरना कोरी कुँवारी चाय चूम के देखो
महकी महकी साँसों से जब नाक छूयेगी
पता चलेगा___ अच्छी चाय क्या होती है !

गुलज़ार

Contents

[1]The history of tea dates back to ancient China, almost 5,000 years ago. Shen Nung named the brew 'ch'a', the Chinese character meaning, to check or investigate, In 200 BC, an emperor of the Han Dynasty ruled that when referring to tea, a special written character must be used illustrating wooden branches, grass, and a man between the two. This written character also pronounced 'ch'a' symbolized the way tea brought humankind into balance with nature for the Chinese culture. Please see www.coffeeteawarehouse.com. For the etymology of the word tea, please see https://en.wikipedia.org/wiki/Etymology_of_tea

'Look at that tea bush, keep looking, keep looking...it is a hundred years old. Yet it sustains so many lives... and will continue to do so.'

When Gordon Fox, ex-chairman of the Goodricke Group Limited, said this in his speech to the shareholders, he was paying tribute to a humble plant that has changed the ways of the world. And of the company he headed.

And indeed, the bush has proved itself one of nature's marvellous creations, that has welded itself into a strong kinship with Man, which has held and grown through the centuries.

Though history acknowledges the fact that tea was probably first discovered as a drinkable beverage with a unique taste in China, India stakes its own claim to fame where both the discovery and cultivation of tea are concerned.

The Chinese legend attributes the discovery of the tea leaf and its properties to Emperor Shen Nong whose rule, 5,000 years ago, was marked by statesmanship and his love of arts and science. Aware of the need for clean drinking water, he advised his subjects to boil water before drinking it. And much as, in the story by Charles and Mary Lamb, crackling pig was discovered as a delicacy when a young boy tried to rescue a suckling pig from a fire in the pigsty, burnt his fingers and stuck them into his mouth to discover a delicious taste, tea was also discovered by serendipity.

According to the story, when the soldiers were boiling the emperor's drinking water, some leaves fell in from a nearby bush. Colour soon leeched from the leaves into the water. Curious about what the leaves could be, the emperor drank the brown liquid to discover he quite liked the taste. Even more delightful was the fact that it made him feel invigorated. And, voila! Tea began to be served as a refreshing liquid, and soon, boiling the green leaves and drinking the infusion became a national habit. The Chinese called the new drink te or ch'a, depending on the region. And till date, countries across the world use variations of these words to describe a drink that they have adapted to their own tastes.[1]

Hello India

How the tea plant, indigenous to China – if legend is to be believed – travelled to India is a story wrapped in mystery. Sufficient to say that some of the nomadic tribes from China fled the country when the Han Chinese gained prominence. Through successive migrations, the people of the Singhpho tribe moved southward, occupying places in Burma and in the north-eastern states of present-day India, including Arunachal Pradesh and some northern areas of Assam.

Whether the hero of our story – the tea bush – grew in Assam too, as it did in China or whether the tribals carried the plants with them when they came might have remained a matter of conjecture, but for discoveries that would soon settle the matter firmly. However, the fertile soil of the region nourished the shrubs and helped them grow into trees. The Singphos knew enough to keep the tea plants pruned to a height at which the leaves could be plucked easily to create their brew. The system they followed was simple. The tender leaves were plucked and dried in the sun. Once dry, they would be exposed to the dew for three nights. The leaves would then be placed inside a hollow bamboo, and the cylinder exposed to the smoke of the fire. In some fortuitous way, the tribe had discovered the technique that was close to what is still being followed to cure the leaf for long-term storage.

Tea would have remained an exotic tribal concoction had it not been for the intrepid British.

Though he was no king, a Scotsman named Robert Bruce shared one trait with his more legendary namesake, who found inspiration in watching a spider climbing up a wet wall. When he discovered tea bushes growing wild in Assam, while he was travelling on a trading mission, he decided to trail it to plunder the riches it might yield. The year was 1823. Doggedly he pursued his quest. His enquiries led him to Maniram Barua, an Assamese who was well regarded by the British and whom he served at that time. Barua was already aware of the fact that the Singhpho tribe cultivated and drank tea. His advice was simple: Bruce should visit the tribal chief Bessa Guam and acquaint himself with the mysteries of tea cultivation.

Can you imagine the scene? The British army major meeting the tribal chief in the remote village. Perhaps each a bit wary of the other, yet the tribal chief hospitable and setting down food and drink for his guest. And tea, of course, in response to his guest's queries.

Bruce leaves peacefully, carrying with him leaves and seeds, spoils from his trip that he places with some pride before the administrators of the East India Company that is gaining ground in the region, and whom he indirectly serves.

A tea plucker hurriedly makes her way home before the sun dips into the horizon in Orangajuli, Assam.

The spoils of Bruce's visit are sent to the Calcutta Botanical garden for an expert horticulturist's verdict. The response from scientist Dr Nathaniel Wallace comes soon enough. Yes, it is tea. But no, not the kind that grows in China. The local variety may not be good enough for the British to bother themselves with.

If Robert Bruce was disappointed, there is no record of it. What history does tell us is that he died before a second opinion could be garnered about the importance of his discovery. It remained to Charles Bruce, his brother, to pursue the trail. Charles Bruce would plant tea around his bungalow, determined to find acceptance for his brother's discovery.

History records that in later years, seeing how the British dealt summarily with the Ahom rulers he owed allegiance to, Maniram Barua turned into a

revolutionary. Though he is reported to have set up tea gardens of his own, there is no account of the British regarding it as important or of Barua offering any information about it to them either.

But realizing the soil of the Assam plains were fertile enough to suit the planting of tea, the East India Company ensures to make the most of it. It undertakes the task of demonstrating 'the practicality of producing tea – thereafter, it would be for private companies to pursue the matter'. It is an ambitious plan. The journey from Calcutta to the thickly forested regions of Assam, where tea is most likely to grow, takes an estimated four months. Danger from wild animals is a further impediment. But with the zeal of explorers out on a mission to tame the wilds, the British set out to realize their plan.

Young tea plants thrive under tender care in a nursery in Goodricke's Aibheel gardens in West Bengal.

Charles Bruce is now recruited for the job in 1835, many years after his brother first met the Singhpho chief. A year later, Charles resigns from his army commission and officially takes up the office of the superintendent of the Assam tea plantations. His salary is Rs 400. His job is to supervise, along with another tea hunter, Lt Charlton, the establishment and nurturing of tea nurseries assigned to a scientific team that included the scientist Wallace.

Bruce was a man of many parts and took to his new assignment showing he was quick to adapt, understand and apply. Two reports by him sent to his superiors show how methodically he went about his task, laying the roots of what today is one of Assam's greatest cash crops.

A report in the Chambers Edinburgh Journal dated Saturday, 25 January 1840[2] quoting from a report by Charles Bruce dated Jaipore, 10 June 1839 not only mentions that 'Mr C.A. Bruce, (who it appears made this discovery fourteen years ago) was immediately appointed by the committee to survey the district and report on its capabilities of producing the plant, under culture', but goes on to clarify that 'the districts of Muttock and Singpho, to which Mr Brace's inquiries have as yet been confined, lie between the 26th and 28th degrees of north latitude, and the 94th and 96th degrees of east longitude, a situation corresponding, in one important respect, to the best tea-districts in China, which lie between the 27th and 31st parallels.' More significant is the line that proclaims, 'Mr Bruce has now found a hundred and twenty such tracts. They are all on plains...' referring to areas where tea plants were found in abundance.

The British lost no time. Realizing that the Chinese tea plant had high regards worldwide, Bruce was given the task of planting seeds and plants from China. These could be grown in their natural form, in the fertile land. Or so they thought. But nature has her own ways. The plants cross pollinated with the indigenous crop, and the yield proved bitter and unpalatable.

In a second report by Charles Bruce that has significance for this historical perspective, the man proves his enquiring and alert mind. Titled 'An Account of the Manufacture of the Black Tea, As Now Practised at Suddeya in Upper Assam, by the Chinamen Sent Thither for That Purpose', the report through dialogues with the Chinamen and his own observations traces the planting and tending of tea in China and the preparation of the leaves for brewing. The report stands as a benchmark, even today, of the process that the leaf goes through in factories in Assam, and perhaps elsewhere, to become what we know as black tea.

Even while he learnt the process of converting the green leaves into a drinkable brew, Bruce was contemplating ways of growing tea in Assam that would be of better quality than what the Chinese plants were offering up at that time. In a section in the same report titled 'A few Observations on the Tea Plant of Assam', he writes:

---

[2]Chambers Edinburg Journal, Volume 9, No. 417, https://books.google.co.in/books?redir_esc=y&id=d7MaAQAAMAAJ&q=25+January+1840#v=snippet&q=25%20January%201840&f=false

The Tea [sic] plants in Assam have in general been found to grow, and to thrive best, near small rivers and pools of water, and in those places where, after heavy falls of rain, large quantities of water have accumulated, and in their struggle to get free, have cut out for themselves numerous small channels.

About the middle of last March, I brought three or four thousand young plants from their native soil in the Muttuck country, about eight days journey, and planted them in the tree-jungles of this place, eight and ten close together, in deep shade. From 400 to 500 were planted in different places, some miles from each other; in the latter end of May I visited them and found them as fresh as if they had been in their native soil, throwing out fresh leaves. As these thrived so well, last June I brought from the same place 17,000 more young plants, and planted them in Coor-kah Mutty, about two miles from this place in deep shade; they are now throwing out new leaves and thriving as well as could be expected, although the soil here is nothing like that from whence they were taken – in which point alone the places differ. To show how very hardy they are I may mention that they were in the first instance plucked out by the roots by the village people who were sent to bring them from their native jungles, put upright into baskets without any earth, brought two days journey on men's hacks, put upright into canoes, a little common earth only being thrown amongst their roots, and were from seven to twenty days before they reached me; and then they had to be carried half a day's journey to the intended new plantation, and were four and five days with only a little moist earth at their roots, before they were finally put into the ground. And yet these plants are doing well; at least the greater part of them.

His experiments proved fruitful. When a sample of the tea grown from indigenous plants was finally sent to Calcutta to the tea committee, it is reported that the tea experts heartily approved of the tea and proclaimed it to be of 'good quality'. A report adds: 'By 1837, Bruce had a consignment delivered to the tea committee – the consignment consisted of 46 chests filled with tea from the indigenous plants. The first twelve chests of manufactured tea to be made from indigenous Assam leaf were shipped aboard the Calcutta to the Company's board of directors in London in 1838 and were sold at the London auctions. This paved the way for the formation of the "Bengal Tea Association" in Calcutta and

The tea plantation workers of Nonaipara, Assam, balance their pickings of the day on their heads as deftly as they pluck them.

a first joint-stock tea company, the "Assam Company" in London. On witnessing its success, other companies were formed to take up the cultivation of tea.'[3]

It would not be long before the cup that cheers became an intrinsic part of the English way of life.

[3]Source: www.indiatea.org

Camellia and the Indian Dream

A tea company in Cachar district of Assam, the Sephinjuri Bheem Tea Company (SBTC), was running a single tea garden, which was established in 1889 and whose owner traded in the British stock exchange. Gordon Fox realized that this was actually an opportunity for growth. In the early 1950s, Fox quickly invested in a stake in the company; it was small but would prove significant. Serendipity ensured he would also be introduced to Alex Lawrie and Co. SBTC's managing agents in Calcutta. The men struck up a cordial relationship that would bear fruit in the years ahead.

In 1964, the owner sold off his garden, but he retained SBTC. It would be a vehicle to collect a growing portfolio of Indian tea companies. By now, the name had changed to one more suited to its product. Camellia, as the company was now called, took inspiration for its name from the botanical name of the tea plant, Camellia sinensis.

Steadily growing, Camellia bought significant stakes in two venerable Indian tea companies, Alex Lawrie and Co., and Walter Duncan and Goodricke, which had been functioning since the nineteenth century. When the three companies merged in 1967 under the name Walter Duncan and Goodricke name (WDG), Camellia morphed into a full-fledged commercial enterprise from being merely an investment company. It would now own and run a number of diverse businesses, including tea cultivation. These businesses eventually included Alex Lawrie Limited and Walter Duncan and Goodricke Limited. The tea gardens, which later became the Goodricke Group of Companies constituting the associate companies of Stewart Holl India Ltd, Amgoorie India Ltd and Koomber Tea

Company Ltd, were earlier managed by the WDG group and its affiliate firms.

When in 1973, the Foreign Exchange Regulation Act (FERA) came into effect, Camellia split from Duncan Brothers. In 1977, the Goodricke Group was incorporated in West Bengal, India, as a public limited company, with the objective to cultivate, produce, treat, blend, develop, process, purchase, trade and deal with tea in different forms. A certificate of entitlement was granted by the registrar of companies under the terms of the Companies Act, 1956, and permission was granted for the commencement of the business. On 1 January 1978, the Goodricke Group merged with the Sterling Tea Companies – a group of eight companies, active tea producers in India – owning seventeen gardens across Darjeeling, Jalpaiguri district in West Bengal, and in Assam.

The company continued to grow, and in 1984, the Goodricke Group also acquired a group of closed gardens in Darjeeling, which included Castleton and Margaret's Hope apart from a host of gardens in Kurseong valley, acquisitions that made the group the biggest producers of the coveted Darjeeling tea. Though many of the gardens in the Darjeeling area were revived and were later sold, 'the trial and error which took place in those years resulted in two gems being polished to near perfection and today Castleton and Margaret's Hope stand out as quality beacons of Darjeeling orthodox tea', says Shaibal Dutt. Camellia Plc also owns a majority share in Kakuzi Plc, a Kenya-based listed company that grows, manufactures and markets tea, among other farm-based activities.

The gardens of Margaret's Hope stand out as one of the quality beacons of Darejeeling orthodox tea.

Nature's Gift to Man

Across the stretching acres that spread like an emerald carpet, the tea bushes glisten in the changing light. Every bush is of the same height, whether the land is flat or undulating gently; only the colours sometimes vary in tone from dark to lighter shades.

A hardy plant, the tea bush, tended so as to remain dwarfed so the leaves are within plucking height, stands on sturdy legs that burrow deep into the soil. Some, venerable, are gnarled and knotted and bear the signs of their age, but their leaves belie the years, and shine with youthful good health.

Nature is bounteous in its offerings to all living creatures. Fruits feed birds, animals and humans alike, branches offer shade, and trees let their juices be tapped as rubber or resin, and willingly shed their bark should man find need of it for shaping things or to extract colour or make medicinal potions from it.

But of all nature's offerings to man, perhaps tea remains the most universal, a drink that elevates the spirit, revitalizes the body and is a great symbol of hospitality and comfort.

Little wonder the tea garden is one of man's most coveted and cared for properties.

Across the Goodricke gardens that range from the fertile plains of the Dooars to Assam and the world-famous tea-growing slopes of Darjeeling, the tea plant is protected, nurtured and stands as an example of the give and take between man and nature at a level that benefits both, and augurs well for a long-lasting relationship.

A bright yellow wasp rests contentedly among the finest tea leaves of the Badamtam gardens in Darjeeling.

Ensuring the gardens across the group conform to multiple, internationally recognized, certification standards is one way of ensuring that nature is never exploited. 'Sustainability has always been our key mantra,' says Amar Singh Nain, vice-president, operations, Goodricke group, who is personally involved with certification.

Nain traces the involvement of the group with sustainability much before the certifications were put into effect. 'There was a strong awareness in the group about the need to protect nature; it is vital as we have such premium teas, so we had started ensuring all norms were met. However, we did it for ourselves and kept a low profile.

'The idea of applying for the Rain Forest Certification came up only in 2007-08 as we realized that getting the certificate would raise us to a new level, a higher platform. And there was no cost involved. We can now claim and prove

The Goodricke tea gardens of Orangajuli, Assam, are rain-forest certified.

we follow sustainable farming practices, including conservation of biodiversity, ensuring sustainable livelihoods for our workers, conservation of natural resources, and effective management of farms and gardens, and we are the first group in Darjeeling to have all our gardens rain forest certified. Besides this, the Orangajuli and Nonaipara gardens in Assam and the Danguajhar, Leesh River, Chalouni and Meenglas gardens in the Dooars are also rain forest certified.'

Other certifications he mentions with considerable pride include the USDA Organic Certification that gives a company the right to label and sell a product as organic, which is a certificate two of the Goodricke gardens, Badamtam and Barnesberg in Darjeeling, boast of.

The UTZ Certification by S.J.S. Australia Pty Ltd certifies that the garden bearing the certificate upholds 'sustainable farming with better opportunities for farmers, their families and our planet', guaranteeing that the stated social, environmental and economic criteria for tea production have been met.

Besides these, the Darjeeling-based gardens of Thurbo, Badamtam and Barnesberg also claim fair trade certification, that 'emphasises on equality in the marketplace, a partnership between consumer and producer'.

Thurbo, Badamtam, Barnesberg, Orangajuli and Nonaipara gardens also bear the Food Safety System Certification (FSSC 22000) that defines requirements for integrated processes that work together to control and minimize food safety hazards.

Nain lists a number of best practices the group's gardens follow. They include the protection of flora and fauna, limited use of pesticides that are aimed only at specific pests, nurturing of man-made and natural forests, and the creation of fuel bodies. He adds that the group is sensitive to the fact that the gardens share space with wild animals ranging from elephant herds to leopards and wolves, to monkeys and bats, to name a few. This sensitivity is instilled in the vast workforce across the gardens. 'Considering the workforce is made up of many ethnic groups with very different practices and attitudes towards animals and birds, we have had a lot of teaching to do,' he adds.

A tea plantation worker from Lakhipara, West Bengal, pauses to pose with an endearing smile.

Burning Bright

We, writer and photographer, are on our way to the Dooars, after landing in the Siliguri airport. It is a long drive and not always fun, as traffic sometimes clogs the road. However, we have many questions and they keep tumbling out. Mainly about how much the gardens have changed over the years.

Lalit Sinha, general manager and visiting agent, has been entrusted with the task of accompanying us through the gardens we have been assigned to visit in the Dooars region. The West Bengal landscape is soothing: green fields of paddy alternate with golden mustard stretches, and an occasional garden bearing tea flashes past. It all seems innocuous enough.

But obviously, life in the gardens is different from life along the towns. Sinha regales us with stories of his early days as assistant manager. Most of the senior management at Goodricke, starting with Atul Asthana, the MD, began their career from scratch, joining the company fresh out of college, and staying on. Many others have come in after retiring from defence or security services... the discipline and the quiet life beckons them and gives enough scope for administrative skills. Sinha is a combination of both... his family is entrenched in defence, but he is a 'tea man'!

He had just joined the gardens and shared a room with another recruit, who had joined a few months earlier. 'We were too junior to have cars at our service and rode around the garden on bicycles,' he tells us. 'And, at times, I would walk; it is a really good place to walk about, the air is fresh and everything is so green and soothing to the eyes.'

'One evening, while cycling down a slope, I thought I saw a flash of orange ahead of me. I could make no sense of it. I moved closer still, quite jauntily,

A cyclist makes his way through the Meenglas tea gardens at dusk.

unaware of what was waiting there on my path. The flash of orange became two or three stripes, and before I knew it, I was within sight of a large Royal Bengal tiger, standing majestically across my path. I think I nearly died of fright. But the animal ignored me, and just walked. Anyway, I played safe and took another route back.' Sinha has had many more animal encounters during the years since his first sighting, but luckily, with no harm coming to either him or the beast.

The Goodricke tea gardens of Danguajhar, West Bengal, make for picture-perfect postcards.

In Search of Wildlife

Day three of our whistle-stop tour of gardens, where we are treated like royalty by each of the senior managers who play host, sees us rattling along barely there roads, seeking elephants. A 300-strong herd has been reported at Lakhipara. It is not a sight we want to miss; we can quite imagine the impact the photograph will have, if we manage to get one, for the book.

Elephants have a way of being invisible, silent. Often, people who encounter them talk about how they find one standing close enough to touch, having approached soundlessly. In the greenest of surroundings, their dark mass can seem to disappear unless you are extremely sharp-sighted.

Our drive is a dramatic one. Navneet Krishan, our host at Lakhipara, shows us a series of houses along the road, which the elephants have destroyed. A roof has been peeled off, and an entire wall is missing. Luckily, it was not living quarters, but an Integrated Child Development Services (ICDS) structure where children were fed khichadi. Yet, we see lines of cottages along the road and can only hope no elephants decide to visit them. 'Some solar lights have been put up to help spot herd movement,' he said, 'after an elephant crushed a sleeping man's head.'

The Lakhipara gardens are in two parts, with a highway dividing it. Characteristic of this garden are the endless, neat rows of silver oak trees that line the roads, standing like graceful maidens to welcome visitors. Soothing to the eye and a pretty break from the endless rows of low green land formed by tea plants, it makes the garden picturesque indeed.

It lies bang in the midst of the elephant district. The pachyderms come in from further north, from as far as the Manas wildlife sanctuary in Assam, sometimes give birth here and go back. At times, great damage is caused by a

The structure in Lakhipara that was the target of attack by elephants.

young male who stays back and goes into musth. Small families of elephants often hangs around in the jungles in and around the gardens, so it is inadvisable to take evening walks, says Krishan; one may walk straight into a beast as it ambles along on its evening constitutional. Damage, he says, happens when man encounters beast and reacts in fear. So the garden has men who track spoor and warn the labour to keep away from areas where the elephants could be moving in.

Of course all this talk raises our expectations. So we drive along, eyes peeled. But it is all to no avail. Krishan has posted men along the known routes that elephants prefer, and he often stops to check. Finally, after we have crisscrossed the gardens in vain, one of the scouts informs us that there is a group of animals, about six, but they are hidden deep in the forest inside the garden.

Much as we would love to see them and take photographs, the danger is obvious. We drive cautiously around, but the elephants do not show themselves; they seem to have simply vanished.

A scout points to the area where the elephants were last seen.

There is a good chance they may wander back at night, causing red alerts all across the garden, so we are advised not to stay overnight at Lakhipara. Which is a pity because we have discovered common ground with Sangeeta Krishan and would have loved to compare notes with her. She works as a student counsellor for schools and her daughter works with Vogue. Before evening falls, we drive back to spend a second night at Meenglas, another of the company's gardens in the Dooars, the only place where we spend two nights in a row. And quite gladly as the Bajars, our wonderful hosts in their magnificent bungalow, are excellent company.

Elephants are a common sight across all the tea gardens of West Bengal and Assam, as the region is one of their natural habitats. As happens with agriculture, in setting up the tea gardens, man has encroached on the spaces that were once the preserve of elephants. So it is but natural that they wander in and out, seeking to reclaim their space, or in search of food or water.

True to its philosophy of coexisting peacefully with the animal population that shares the regions Goodricke has its gardens in, the practice is to ensure the elephants come and go in peace. Their sightings are cause for alarm, but only action that warns residents – both staff and labour – of animal movement, which works towards preventing damage to life and limb, is taken.

'Herds often come from the forest wilds into the gardens seeking shelter and water,' according to Nigel D'Souza who, at the time of our visit, was the manager of the Nonaipara gardens in Assam. The area around his gardens is rich with wild life, and avid photographer D'Souza's camera has captured Nilgai and spotted deer, barking deer as well as many species of birds and reptiles. This is his second stint at the garden, and D'Souza is happy as he can add to the collection he and his photographer friend created during the first posting. 'We have eighty-three species of butterflies,' D'Souza says proudly.

'When you see an elephant, the natural instinct is to throw stones at it, and that in turn cause further conflict. In 2011, we had the highest record of human deaths due to elephants. We need to change the scenario, to save both man and animal, and I am working towards that.'

Like most of the managers across the group, D'Souza is gung-ho about co-existing with animals and sharing the garden spaces with them in a mutual-benefit plan. Rampant deforestation during the Bodo agitation has robbed the animals of their natural habitat, depleting sources of food and water. The story is the same along all the gardens we visited in Assam. Many herds moved further north into the Bhutan hills, while others, like lost children, roam around, between the forest and the garden.

A characteristic of the Lakhipara gardens are the rows of silver oak trees that line the roads.

'They find shelter in the forests within our gardens,' D'Souza explains. 'They come there, sometimes even give birth, and return. Have you ever seen an elephant herd escorting a new born into the forest?' he asks excitedly, adding, 'It is an amazing sight, the way the females surround and protect the calf as they move along.'

Taking the work of his predecessor forward, D'Souza is furthering a huge awareness programme among the labour to respect the animals and coexist peacefully with them through their comings and goings.

'When you see an elephant, the natural instinct is to throw stones at it, and that in turn causes further conflict. In 2011, we had the highest record of human

deaths due to elephants. We need to change the scenario, to save both man and animal, and I am working towards that.'

Setting up groups of activists is the first step. Forty-five per cent of the labour in the gardens under his care is Hindu, and 'I am explaining the relationship of Ganesha to the elephant, and why it was chosen to portray the qualities of the gods.' It is making a difference, he adds. 'Earlier there would be damage to anything between forty-five to a hundred homes by elephants every year; now it has reduced to two or three.'

He has tracked the movement of elephants, and the corridors they take through the garden are clearly marked in words and visuals. Bright bougainvillaea plants are planted along the corridors; they flower through the year and the labour knows now that the plants signify they are walking where elephants tread. So even if moving herds knock down the boards, they have an additional warning sign in the plants. 'We have a no-interference policy. The animals usually come running into the garden, but once they are inside the gates, they slow down and pad quietly along the roads, causing no harm to the tea plants, and enter the jungle areas. They seek out waterholes in the jungle areas. Sometimes in the heat of summer, we find the waterholes running dry, and,' he says, pointing out wet hollows in the rough ground beside the jeep we are taking a round in, 'we create drinking holes and fill them with water.'

Often in the drains that run along the garden patches to runoff excess water from the planted area, baby elephants get stuck. It causes a lot of furore, with rescue attempts by the older animals and men adding their bit. To prevent such mishaps, the slopes into the drains have been made u-shaped from the traditional sharp v-shaped drop. Every little bit counts.

Recruiting from the labour and garden executives, a core committee of ten has been created of which the garden manager, regardless of who he is, is the president. The core committee includes tea pluckers. 'We are formulating a plan of action and will slowly spread awareness across the gardens and villages. The plan is to include ten villages by next year, and keep widening the circle of awareness,' he explains. And the move is to get the labour groups to take ownership of the programme, elect their leaders by rotation, and increase the number of such groups so each village has its own.'

Keeping a census of the elephant herds also helps. D'Souza has counted 235. 'Twice a year, elephant herds combine, and the line stretches from the forest to halfway across to the next garden of Orangajuli,' he says.

A lone elephant weaves his way through the Goodricke gardens in Orangajuli, Assam.

Welcome the Maharaj

Of the many stories recounted by Lalit Sinha to sweeten the long and tiring drives from one garden in the Dooars to the next, this one is worth the retelling.

'I was quite new in the gardens and shared a house with another young junior manager. One evening, as we were sitting inside, the watchman came to tell us that Maharaj had arrived. "Maharaj aya," he said. I looked at my colleague somewhat intrigued, and he reassured me that it was a blessing to have the venerable sage visit us. "Call him in," I said immediately, "let us make him welcome." The watchman looked a bit taken aback. And my friend said, "That is not how you do it." He handed me a spoon, and said, "you have to go outside and tap him gently with the spoon and invite him in." Quite mystified, I took the spoon from him, and he signalled me to go out. I stepped out of the door to see a huge elephant standing there.

'Rushing in, I told my friend, "There is an elephant outside." He said, "I know, elephants are addressed as Maharaj here. So go and tap his flank with the spoon and ask him to go away. He will go peacefully."

'I went out again, holding the spoon outstretched in readiness. But the elephant was huge, and I lost my nerve and retreated inside. "I can't do it," I said, and my friend rolled on the bed with laughter. "Thank God you did not. Were you really planning it?" he exclaimed. Phew, I told myself, I had a narrow escape. Sometimes fear is a good thing.'

Forests in the Gardens

When the gardens were first created, forests were cleared, and the land made hospitable enough to nurture the tea plants that were planted in neat, endless rows. The plantations caused colonies of workers to settle within and around the periphery, pluckers, gardeners, and a host of other skilled and semi-skilled labour who came with their families to earn their livelihood working in the gardens.

'Over the years the new settlements took their toll on the surrounding forests,' says Subroto Sen, whose stately home is our refuge during our visit to Badamtam in the Darjeeling hills. The forests were an easy source of firewood for cooking and keeping warm, and the depletion was faster than nature's capacity to renew the growth.

Over the years, in every garden, with sustainability as the ruling mantra, afforestation has been underway in an attempt to give back to nature what she has lost. Most gardens plant indigenous trees in the areas around, as well as within the gardens, and also demarcate areas where they grow trees for fuel. The fuel tree plantations are divided into sections, which are quickly replanted to ensure a regular supply. 'When we cut down 5,000, we plant 10,000, but the long-term aim is to ensure all labour gets gas connections,' Amar Singh Nain says.

In Badamtam, for one, this has already been achieved. Hundred per cent of the labour has gas connections. And all the fuel trees have grown to create forested areas, adding to the dense forests that have been planted around. 'Actually, even from Barnesberg, you can see the thick forests here,' we are told.

Homes of tea pluckers nestle between the trees in Darjeeling, West Bengal.

The garden rules strictly prohibit the uprooting or cutting of trees, whether indigenously grown or planted by man. The trees remain an important ally of the tea gardeners. They provide shade and protect the shrubs from too much sun even as they make plucking less taxing for the labour. But a balance needs to be carefully maintained.

On the first day of our visit to the Dooars, J.C. Pande, senior manager, Danguajhar, explained to us much of the delicate machinery that tea garden managers have to keep in motion between nature and man to ensure maximum output. As we drive around and sometimes walked through the narrow divisions between one square of plants and the next, stopping to take pictures, Pande tells us about the interdependence between the trees and the plants. 'While we need shade for the tea plants, we must ensure they don't get too much shade,' he says, adding that ideally, there should be around 40 per cent sunlight to keep bacterial and fungal contamination at bay. Too little shade will wither the plants, too much

The view after the mist lifts on a rainy morning in the Goodricke gardens of Badamtam, West Bengal.

will cause other problems. He points to trees that have been marked. These, he explains, are giving more than the required amount of shade, and their branches will be logged off. Sometimes an entire tree may be cut, but that is only when it is absolutely necessary. 'All of it requires regular monitoring,' he says.

Little wonder then, to cover gardens that stretch across 900 or more hectares in some cases, managers, however senior, must take regular rounds. Most start at 5.30 or 6.00 as dawn turns to light, to return for breakfast. Subsequent rounds could be two or three in number.

As we accompany each of our hosts on their post-breakfast rounds, and again in the late afternoon before dusk falls, the real spirit of adventure each must

carry in their hearts makes itself evident. The ride is not only gruelling on the mud roads, but also dusty and can be uncomfortably hot or cold, depending on the time of the year. The monsoons bring their own problems, turning the mud to slush, capable of stranding a vehicle. But come rain or shine, the tours around the garden are the only way the person in charge can ensure all is well. The labour, plants, animals and profits are all part of a manager's duties, and the work never stops 365 days a year.

Trees also play the role of sentinels, warning of pests that could be inhabiting their bark and pose a serious threat to the tea plantations. Each garden has devised its own way of setting up an alarm system against pests. Using stands or the trunks of the trees within the garden, planters wrap a sticky sheet and shine a light that mimics moonlight. Moths attracted to the light get caught in it. It is one way to be abreast of egg hatching time and be warned of caterpillar infestation, we are told. The strips of sticky material are usually blue or white. Red scares birds and so is never used.

The blue sticky sheets wrapped around the trees attract pests that would otherwise attack the tea leaves. It also serves to alert the garden about the breeding season. It's a cleaner way to deal with pests and lessens the dependence on pesticides.

Fighting Unseen Enemies

'Pest infestation is a real challenge for the planter,' A. Sengupta, wholetime director and CFO of Goodricke at the Calcutta HO, says. 'Between 2003 and 2004 pest activity went up enormously ... and the cost per hectare rose by about four to five times what it had been in 2000. It was a real struggle to control and bring down the costs.'

One of the decisions taken by the group was to attack the problem without causing any threat to the environment. Increasing use of pesticides would have been contrary to the sustainability and the organic parameters.

In Danguajhar tea estate, a quiet operation is on to ensure the war against pests is won without any doubt. Kalpana Sharma, who joined the Research and Development (R&D) section in 2011, introduces us to the wards she has been nurturing in her laboratory.

The contents of the large bottles ranged on the shelves are anything but pretty, in fact, they might even be called revolting, but they are powerful armour against the denizens who come with full intent of devouring leaf and bud and destroying the estate's precious contents.

'We use micro-organisms to lower the usage of chemicals in the gardens,' Sharma explains. So we gaze at a fungus called tricoderma, which she is using to make a bio-pesticide. This is powerful against 'red rust' as well as many other diseases that attack tea plants, she explains.

Kalpana Sharma and an assistant at work in the laboratory in Dangaujhar, West Bengal.

'Nature helps keep us in business by offering us the hardy tea plant and the least we can do is to protect her and keep her healthy'

Using bio-fertilizers that carry nitrogen-fixing bacteria, or another that helps fix phosphate and other available nutrients from soil to plant, she hopes to eliminate chemical fertilizers completely. For now, her mission is to 'multiply these in immense quantities' so that all the Dooars gardens can benefit, beside the three gardens in Darjeeling that are already getting certain amounts for use.

Soil testing to know the health of the soil– proportions of potassium, sulphur, phosphorous and to determine the pH– factor helps decide if the calorific value is high, indicating fertile soil for the plants to thrive in. The ash quantum should be low, she adds.

Cultures are placed in a big vessel and multiplied by agitation and aeration that cause fermentation. At optimum temperature large quantities of bacteria can be produced. These are sprayed instead of chemical products. Other bio-products used include cow urine, which is sent to other gardens also.

Nigel D'Souza carries out his own experiments towards sustainable and eco-friendly warfare against pests. He has put his garden staff on a watch to see which plants the pests are repelled by and is using those plants to protect tea plants. To his delight, 'some of it works well indeed.'

Of course, such measures are wont to push the costs higher. Sengupta admits: 'Our average prices are far higher than the district average, by Rs 20 to Rs 30 a kg. But our buyers know we stand for sustainability and high quality with no compromise, so they come to us.'

'Nature helps keep us in business by offering us the hardy tea plant and the least we can do is to protect her and keep her healthy,' says Sengupta, and why not, when it results in a win-win for both sides.

A signature spider weaves its trademark web amongst the leaves of the Badamtam tea gardens.

Time Travel in the Darjeeling Hills

Margaret's Hope, deep in the hills of Darjeeling, has the most romantic name. And there is a sweet story about it. But more of that later.

Samir Ranjan Gupta, the manager whose house we are stationed in for the day after our arrival the previous evening, has planned a surprise. The house itself is one that wants to hold us back. There is something about the large rooms, the memorabilia on the walls and the view of the vistas below, all the way across the valley and to the hills fairly beyond, all of which makes us want to just dawdle around and take it all in. But Gupta has a plan. And it includes a surprise.

So we clamber on to his trusty steed that toils its painful way up the rough, steep road that leads out from his house to the world outside. And I can sense his suppressed excitement as we drive through the winding slopes of the gardens. The rain has visited us the night before, and the tea leaves glisten in the watery light. As we slow down at times to change gears, or let a line of tea pluckers pass, I spot white flowers on some of the bushes by the roadside. Pretty flowers with soft broad petals and a yellow centre, they remind me of camellia or maybe gardenia. But I am no botanist, and these are the flowers nature has gifted to the tea plant.

Steep slopes await us, through narrow roads that get narrower. I get no response to my questions on where we are going. I have an inkling as I remember a conversation earlier on, when the list of our explorations of the garden was being discussed. I suspect we are going to look at some old-world denizen of the region, whose ancestors go back to the Jurassic Age, the salamander.

The salamander moves sluggishly, allowing plenty of time for photographs.

Before starting on this book, I have read up about the salamander, and now know from Wikipedia that 'the earliest known salamander fossils have been found in geological deposits in China and Kazakhstan, dated to the middle Jurassic period around 164 million years ago.' I also know that there are 655 living species of salamander, scattered across the globe, and they can vary in size from many feet to a few inches. And I learn, to my dismay, that as with all creatures great and small, this remnant of evolution that has survived millions of years, is on the threatened list, at least some of the species are.

When accosted with the question if we are going to see salamanders, Gupta smiles mysteriously. But the mystery is soon solved. We turn steeply down a muddy road and draw up near a lake.

It is, to put it briefly, a beautiful spot. The light is perfect, and photographs are in order. But the main attraction is waiting.

Gupta tells us the story of the lake, known locally as the Salamander Bhanjyang Lake. A man-made lake, created by L. Hanagann, manager of Margaret's Hope Tea Estate, in 1947, it was thrown into disuse after an accident in 1955 when a boy, out rowing on the lake, drowned when his boat capsized. Fear, superstition and neglect ensured the lake was subsequently shunned. It was soon overgrown by weeds and vegetation, and nature was in the process of claiming it back. Which could have been well enough, especially for the salamanders who inhabited the area.

But in 1968, a disastrous landslide threatened even more dire calamities, and a move was made to correct the imbalance. Heavy rainfall caused a nick on one end of the reservoir, channelling the water out, risking it draining away. Murmurs about restoring the lake that was fast turning into a swamp finally turned to action in 2003, when the authorities of the Margaret's Hope tea garden joined hands with the local village panchayat headed by Jagat Sangbo. The process revealed a large community of salamanders in the area, and the lake was soon dubbed Gora Bari by the Nepalese, as Gora meant salamander and Bari was the word for home. Some studies about the salamanders of the lake were initiated and they gained a lot of attention. It was not long after that the Himalayan salamander, to which these creatures belonged, was listed under the endangered and protected category of the Indian Wildlife (Protection) Act of 1972.

Sangbo proved a visionary, who could motivate members of twenty-five other panchayats to volunteer their services to the job at hand, and with a minimum cost of Rs 60,000, the lake was shining in the sunlight once again by 2005 and teeming with fish soon after. A new embankment was built – higher than the original one, with three piped outlets – which ensured the safety of the lake.

Perhaps the revitalizing of the lake was indeed a blessing for the Jurassic-age residents of the area, for Gupta tells us that a careful recording of their numbers has shown they are steadily, though slowly, growing.

Goodricke has been protecting the salamander since 1990. It supported the then principal of the Darjeeling Government College, Prof. B. Dasgupta, who was studying the salamanders under a WWF project, which was sponsored by Goodricke.

We also learn that Darjeeling and Manipur are the only areas in India where this amazing creature lives. We hope to see one, we say, but knowing how shy they are, might well be disappointed.

We are not. Gupta has made all arrangements, and a worker stands waiting, with a salamander trapped for us to take a look at.

It is a black, lizard-like creature, with short legs. I think of the lizard and the crocodile, but unlike both species that can move at amazing speeds when they put their mind to it, this one moves with quiet deliberation. Once let out of the net that holds it, on to a rock, it moves sluggishly, allowing plenty of time for photographs. Then, as we watch, it wanders off towards the forested thickets.

Gupta tells us the salamanders in that region alternate between the water

The 'best selfie point' at Margaret's Hope, West Bengal.

'The garden has already formed the Protect Salamander Group that is undertaking work that includes creating awareness among the people of surrounding villages about the importance of protecting these unique creatures.'

and the land and are protected by the locals as well as the gardens. Since the Goodricke group has taken up the protection of the area, boating and other such activities are not encouraged. Anyway, the natural silting of the lake has made it less attractive for such pursuits.

As the introduction of fish to be bred for local consumption by villagers has threatened the salamander, Goodricke has built a smaller pond where the eggs of this amphibian can be saved from becoming fish food and can hatch safely. This has proved to be a big helping hand to the continued survival of this rare species.

A second initiative that has proved necessary is the building of soak pits to prevent human waste and dirty water flowing down into the lake and polluting it with chemicals. Further initiatives include regular desilting, building of a small dam to prevent cracks in the restraining walls, and the construction of sidewalls and a fence to prevent pisciculture, as it threatens the salamander's continued existence.

The Margaret's Hope garden plans to create an ideal habitat of the rare Himalayan salamanders at a private mini-wildlife sanctuary, to conserve the habitats from local anthropogenic pressure. 'The garden has already formed the Protect Salamander Group that is undertaking work that includes creating awareness among the people of surrounding villages about the importance of protecting these unique creatures,' Gupta says.

We marvel at the ability of this amazing creature, which can recreate and regrow a missing limb or tail, much as a lizard grows its tail back. And I learn much to my surprise that it is a kinsman, not of the lizard as I had imagined, or the crocodile, but of the frog. And more amazing, salamanders are directly descended from the dinosaurs! More important, the salamander, which is also seen in North America, is the subject of deep scientific study to find ways to replicate in man the amphibian's ability to regenerate lost limbs. If this happens, and doctors can find ways of adapting for humans the processes involved in forming new tissue, it could help in healing spinal injuries, repairing damaged organs and limbs in ways that seem miraculous at the present moment.

Awe makes us very quiet as we prepare to leave the place, but Gupta requests us to brave the drizzle that has started and walk along a bit further to what he calls the 'best selfie point'. I am reluctant, as selfies do not feature in our scheme of things, but we are just curious enough to go along. The road ends abruptly in a steep edge, and before us is indeed a wonderful view of gardens laid out in consecutive rings. In the mist of the drizzle, there is a certain magical quality and the image is imprinted into my memory forever to come up whenever I think of Margaret's Hope.

As a passing shot, Gupta adds: 'After converting to gas instead of using fossil fuel and conserving these living fossils, we can truly take pride in being a real green garden, possibly the only one in Darjeeling.'

A Cat Story

Evenings at the Thurbo 'big house', where the general manager, J.D. Rai, stays are quiet affairs. There is no need for entertainment or action, the house overlooks the valley stretching ahead, and from a spot in the garden, one can see a bit of the world-renowned Kanchenjunga peak.

The Rais belong to the region and have been part of the Goodricke gardens of Darjeeling for years. Rai oversees three gardens besides Thurbo.

It is a modest house as manager's houses in tea gardens go, but a charming one. Our room is upstairs, cosy and wooden, and smelling of timbre. Something about the room reaches out to us, reminding of some room we must have been cocooned in during our very disparate childhoods, but both of us yearn all through our visit to Darjeeling to go back to it.

Rain and mist keep interfering with the view, and it looks cold outside, coming as we have from the warmer regions of the Dooars below. But the Rais have ensured the living room is warm.

A vast ground surrounds the house, lined with pretty plants, all of which are withholding their colour for brighter days. Two strong gates barricade the entrance to the grounds. 'It's because of the leopards,' Rai tells us. 'Without the gates, they would just amble in.'

Indeed, leopards have stood in picturesque poses at the edge of the grounds often enough, we are told, as if daring humans, who have usurped what was many generations ago, their exclusive terrain, to chase them away. 'We have learnt to coexist,' Rai says.

Home of the Rais in Thurbo, Darjeeling.

But Sinam Rai, his wife, is not as sanguine about the big cats. Mainly because of her penchant for the smaller, domestic variety.

We watch as her two wards play around the room, tumbling over each other, chasing their tails, climbing and jumping from small heights. It is delightful and even more so when they respond like obedient puppies would to her call. 'Lucy,' she says, and they gambol up to her as she sits on her comfortable sofa, knitting. Both cats are called Lucy, she explains, and they anyway do everything together. At a command, they jump up on to her lap and snuggle down in the welcome warmth.

'They are still babies,' Mrs Rai tells us. 'I just had them for a few months.' But obviously, she has been adopted as surrogate mother.

'However, I have learnt not to get too fond of them,' she adds, 'because invariably the leopards get them. Unlike dogs, cats do not stay inside the house

Sinam Rai sets up a spot in her lawn to serve us a cup of Darjeeling's finest.

howsoever much we try to keep them in, and when they venture out at night, they are a tasty treat for the hunter outside.' For now her wards are too young to want to look for adventure outside. Besides, the rain and mist are strong disincentives. 'But they will grow up,' she adds in a tone of finality.

For now, the Lucys are her loyal companions, following her around and cuddling up when the mood takes any of them to do so.

'We decided to brave it. We laughed loudly – it helped quell the fear – and clutching the iron rods very firmly in our hands, kept walking. The tiger walked away and cleared the road for us. But we had a very tough time not giving in to the urge to run, even after it had gone. Who knew where it was watching us from!'

If the elephant is the main animal preoccupation of the plains, in the mountainous regions of Darjeeling, planters worry about the tiger and the leopard. The former is sighted more rarely now, having learnt to find new haunts higher up into the wildernesses, but the leopard, perhaps tempted by easy prey like dogs and cats and the occasional child who might stray into its precinct, lurks around like a watchful thief.

Joel Lakra, who retired as bearer-cum-driver at the 'big house' in Thurbo, tells his story with gusto of an encounter he survived.

'My parents also lived in the garden,' he says; 'my mother plucked tea, my father was a gardener, and shaped this garden in his own way. My siblings and I were very young when it happened. We were going back from work when we saw it. Luckily, we were carrying iron rods in our hands, as was the practice then, whenever we went out on our own. We stopped when we saw the animal. In turn, it crouched, cat-like, when seeing us. Perhaps it was ready to pounce. My heart stopped I think, but my brain was working, fortunately so. We told each other, "Do not run, though our legs were already signalling flight. Do not run, or the beast will chase us. And it is much faster." But we were scared. Very scared.

'We decided to brave it. We laughed loudly – it helped quell the fear – and clutching the iron rods very firmly in our hands, kept walking. The tiger walked away and cleared the road for us. But we had a very tough time not giving in to the urge to run, even after it had gone. Who knew where it was watching us from!'

His encounters with tigers were many, and once he had to run to the assistant manager's house when a large animal reared its head from the bushes and roared at him. He pleaded with the helpers there for support, but they were too scared. 'But I had to come for work, and the tiger was there on my way. So I told myself, be brave, he is not interested in you, and picking up a huge boulder in case I needed to use it, I went bravely ahead. I shouted loudly as I approached the place where he had been sitting and passed safely through. I think he had moved away.'

Tigers, like the leopards do now, used to pace on the platform in front of the house, or play like kittens on the periphery. Once a tiger had ventured near his house and was growling around, causing his mother to panic and phone him at the 'big house'. 'Luckily, there were no confrontations,' he added.

The tea garden slopes of Thurbo, Darjeeling.

Tea baskets lined up by the roadside in Thurbo, Darjeeling.

Worms as Friends

Self-sufficient mother nature makes her own arrangements for renewal and sustainability when it comes to soil. Among her helpers in this task are the humble earthworm and many other kindred creatures that burrow and rake the soil in a constant movement of replenishment that keeps it moist and fertile. Their own bodies, when they shed waste or die, add to the nutrients. All astute farmers know this and try and make these often unseen and disregarded denizens into strong allies.

At the 890-hectare, 150-year-old Aibheel tea garden, the landscape is picturesque. Soft slopes create visual drama as the tea plants seem to flow in waves along the surface. A morning mist makes it even more poetic, and pleasant to the eyes after the stretches of plains in the other Dooars gardens we have visited. The trees here seem to spread their branches wider, as if holding the spaces in their embrace. 'It looks lovely, yes,' says R.S. Gill, the manager and our host, as we take a round of his garden, 'but it is a tough garden to maintain. Some of the areas are very difficult for the planters to access. In fact, in plenty of places, one cannot even see the shrubs, and we have issues of water stagnation and silting.'

At Aibheel, we are witness to how Goodricke works with nature's helpers to enrich the soil. The compost shed reveals itself to our olfactory senses much before we get close. The mix of compost and active worms is not pleasant to look at either, but Raghunath, one of the gardeners, seems not to notice the fact. To him, it is a job that yields rich results. We watch as a wagonload of tea waste rumbles up and is offloaded. It forms part of the nourishment for the worms, who in turn will turn it into nourishment for the soil.

I learn about the many benefits of this process from the net: 'Because the

The soft slopes of the Aibheel gardens create visual drama as the tea plants seem to flow in waves along the surface.

earthworms grind and uniformly mix minerals in simple forms, plants need only minimal effort to obtain them. The worms' digestive systems create environments that allow certain species of microbes to thrive to help create a "living" soil environment for plants. The fraction of soil which has gone through the digestive tract of earthworms is called the drilosphere.' It does seem like a miraculous regeneration.

Overplaying the stink of compost is the stench of burning rubber. Further down, rubber is being processed from the material that has been tapped from the trees grown on the plantation. 'We plant rubber trees as they are suitable to the area and to the climate,' Gill says. 'It is another way of adding to the garden's income with minimum expense.'

In gardens like Orangajuli, up to two metric tonnes of cow dung is used to augment the efforts of the worms to enrich the soil. It also helps lessen the pesticide load on the environment.

Raghunath poses oblivious to the smells of the compost mix wafting all around us.

Raghunath, who heads the central nursery at Aibheel, takes us on a quick round. He is one of the garden's most loyal employees, passionate about the job he has been entrusted with. 'Some time ago, he suffered a stroke,' Gill tells us. 'But after lying in bed for some days, he forced himself to get up, put on his shoes and began taking rounds of his garden.' Raghunath smiles when he realizes he is being praised. 'I start my rounds at 4.30 in the mornings and take four to six rounds every day; it was how I healed myself,' he adds.

Raghunath exemplifies the typical Goodricke employee across levels. Most of them, whether plucker, clerk, medical assistant or senior executive, have notched up decades of service to the company, with no thought of trying their luck elsewhere.

But Aibheel has other 'stars', one of whom even made it to the *Kaun Banega Crorepati* show. Kaki, as everyone calls her with affection, earned her name as the universal aunt thanks to her cooking for the schoolchildren at the

garden. With the help of just one assistant, today, Kaki cooks for 450 kids, who lick their fingers clean after every meal. She has been at it for the past thirteen years, and her dedication and love earned her a slot at the KBC show, where, like the bright young boy played by Dev in Slumdog Millionaire, Kaki worked her way up the ladder of questions to win the magical one crore rupee prize.

When asked by the quiz master what she wanted most for featuring on the show, she said, 'I want my own mobile, as I am sharing one now with my husband, who works as a peon in the company school.' She was, of course, presented with one, as well as the money that was her rightful haul. 'The money is in her account,' we are told, 'but she has continued her life as if nothing has changed.'

We also meet Tai, whose mothering instinct has obliterated her real name. About thirteen years ago, Tai was forced to sing on railway platforms to be able to feed herself and her ten-day-old baby. By night, defenceless and alone, she would seek refuge in the cremation ground, knowing that fear of ghosts and djinns would keep predatory men away. Somewhere along the way, she started picking up abandoned children and playing mother to them. Today, she has a large number of children whom she cares for.

Aibheel is a good example of how nature can also prove a challenge to man's efforts. It rains heavily in these parts and the slopes suffer much damage, with the rain often washing away soil, and the plants on it. 'The cement borders along the river were washed away,' Gill tells us, explaining the work that is being carried out down below, where stones wrapped in wire meshing are being placed to prevent the river water coming through.

A water tank in Aibheel leaves us with a pertinent message.

Pluckers from Orangajuli, Assam, wait to have their pickings from the morning weighed.

The Human Factor

The tea-leaf plucker is perhaps the most visual aspect of a tea garden, and also its most vital one. Cartons that package tea bags or leaves for the market often have photographs of brightly clad women, with the leaf gathering basket hanging along their back from a strap across their forehead as they smile into the camera. They stand waist-deep amidst the tea bushes, which stretch out in a slope behind them to the edge of the photograph. Very romantic indeed, and perhaps the visual adds its own flavour to the cup one brews.

But the life of a plucker is moored in work that demands patience, fortitude and skill. Like the embroiderer whose unseen hours of labour decorate and embellish the fabric or garment he works on and enables the seller or designer to mark up the price manifold, the tea plucker's expertise lies at the crux of the quality of tea produced. An inexpert plucker could well ruin the best crop from the best plants.

'Perceptions have to change.' Shaibal Dutt is emphatic about this. Sitting across me at his table in his Kolkata office, he shares his views. He thinks the time is right to move the leaf plucker from the 'unskilled' category to being labelled as 'skilled worker'. 'We need to build dignity into labour in the gardens,' he believes. Dutt also has a blueprint for improving the equipment used by the pluckers: better footwear, nicer aprons and head gear ... and posters shot professionally of picture-perfect pluckers that will boost their morale as well as the perception of themselves even as it communicates their importance to the general public. 'It is necessary,' he adds, 'like most skilled but unsung labour, the plucker may soon be on the endangered list.'

Dutt is not alone in this. Increasingly, gardens across the tea belt are beginning to feel the pressure of man versus nature. Nature works like clockwork and

Across the gardens, the picture of the tea plucker differs minimally. While in the Dooars they carry their baskets on the side, in Darjeeling and the northern parts of Assam the more familiar picture of the basket hanging behind the shoulders is what one sees.

Tea pluckers at work on a sunny day in the gardens of Nonaipara, Assam.

presents us with fresh leaves season after season. The leaves must be plucked at just the right time to be able to give us tea of the best quality. But if labour is not there to do the job, the entire enterprise can fail.

At the gardens, we watch the women and men at work. They are in 'uniform', an apron-like shift worn over their regular clothes, their heads covered, a basket for leaves as their only equipment. Their expertise lies in their nimble fingers and eyes. And their ability to pluck, pluck, pluck... just at the right place, so all they nip off from the stem is two leaves and a bud. Sometimes, there are more than two leaves, but that is rare, and skilled and time-tested workers seldom err on this count.

Across the gardens, the picture of the tea plucker differs minimally. While in the Dooars they carry their baskets on the side, in Darjeeling and the northern parts of Assam the more familiar picture of the basket hanging behind the shoulders is what one sees. What sets the hill women apart is their love of colour and the fact that they are able to put away their roles as 'labour' along with their day's work, and don bright clothes, makeup and walk home, their neatly cut hair swinging gaily on their shoulders or down their back. In fact, the Darjeeling workers seem to know they are the elite among their clan, thanks to the leaf that has won worldwide fame for its unique flavour. Their houses are colourfully neat, with TV antennas hoisted on each roof, and they meet our gaze more readily, and flash bright smiles when we stop to chat with them.

A tea plucker's expertise lies in their nimble fingers. Borbam, Assam.

In fact, one enduring visual I have carried back is of the line of women with empty baskets swinging behind them, wending their sure-footed way up a steep slope, half-hidden by the tea bushes. They stand precariously at times on the slopes that hold the bushes and pluck with a nonchalance that amazes the plains dwellers.

Life in the tea garden, for the plucker and Bada Sahib alike, follows nature meticulously. When it is the right time, as winter gives way to the first signs of spring, the dormant tea plants awaken to send out new leaves and buds. The leaves come up all at once and need to be nipped, or the crop is lost. Dutt's own duties include touring the gardens under his care as 'visiting agent' to ensure man and nature are in step. 'Often after a longish winter, everyone has become a bit laid-back through the lean season, and it is easy to miss it if one patch of the garden is waking up and sending out leaves. Someone in the garden all the time may not see it, while an outsider can quickly notice the difference. That is why seniors are asked to make trips across gardens,' he explains. 'Being more experienced, we adopt a supervisory role.'

The most important aspect of tea plucking is to 'catch the first flush on time'. The period, usually in March, could span twenty to twenty-five days at the most. Sometimes additives are sprayed at the close of the flush period to give the plants one last push, before they are allowed to rest again.

During the dormant phase, called banjhi, from the local word for barren, the soil rests; the plant renews itself and gears up for another spurt. Dutt adds that some gardens would at this time spray the plants with additives to shorten the barren stretch.

It is in May, when the sun does its magic, that the tea plant offers it best bouquet. 'In March when the heat rises after the cool of winter, the plants react, and the resultant brew is light,' Dutt explains. 'But the second flush is stronger, richer and more full of flavour. All conditions are right, and the plant has come out of shock to give us the best teas of the season.'

Nature alerts man to the fact that the second flush is ready. The Jarul (*Lagerstroemia speciose*) trees send out pink flowers almost as a signal, the timing mostly coincides with the timing for plucking the second flush. Nature-watchers also see how the leaves across bushes gain a slight yellowish tinge. This is when all the pruned bushes come into bearing stage and give forth leaves that bear a lot of vigour.

It is interesting how planters speak of the bush as an entity that lives and interacts with them, submitting to care and rewarding them with its offering of leaves and buds. Perhaps it is this close association and empathy with the gardens they tend that puts the tea planter in a category of their own, among all planters and farmers. The lonesome life that living in a plantation enforces also creates the intertwining of emotions between nature and man. And it is common to see, whether it be the general manager or the humble plucker, the empathy levels at a high. To me, it adds a certain old-world romance to the tea garden story, which combined with early morning mists and winding mud roads, is almost uniquely

Lunch break in Borbam, Assam.

magical. I know I will never drink a cup of tea anywhere without the visual of a garden of bushes flashing across my mind.

The women pluckers come across as infinitely more interesting than the men. In the plains, like the men, most ride up from their colonies on bikes, carrying their food with them. It is always easy, while driving through the many tracts of plantations inside the vast gardens to know where the plucking is happening; the bicycles leaning against the trees alongside the road are the first giveaway, even if the pluckers are deep inside and almost hidden by the green.

The garden is sectioned off into twenty-six parts, A to Z. Plucking begins in Section A on Monday and moves down alphabetically through the sections so as to return to A by the next Monday. A new leaf has to be plucked within seven days; if it lasts beyond that and is plucked on the eighth, ninth or tenth day, the leaf will be too big, and the quality would have deteriorated. Transportation of newly plucked leaves with minimum time lag, and its handling are the next important aspects workers have to stick to.

Plucking starts very early in the morning, and so lunchtime is earlier than is normal in our urban homes. Lunchtime is when you see the pluckers coming into their own. They stop being automatons, concentrated on moving their fingers so they do not tear or destroy, but only pluck the leaves desired for treatment into tea. The chatter and laughter as they sit cross-legged across the road, to partake of the food they have carried from home, is a heart-warming sight. Of course, when we chance upon them as we drive past in our vehicle, they scatter; picking up their bags and tiffin boxes quickly, but from afar, they create an idyllic picnic scene. It is a happy respite before they go back to their arduous task again that will end when the sun slants downwards to let in the dusk.

'They called the forest car and took me to hospital. It took six months in the Siliguri hospital for me to be able to walk again. My brother works here too, he came and took care of me,' he said, adding, 'but I was taken care of by the company all the while.'

At various points in the garden, water tankers on strong trolleys stand to provide drinking water to workers, so they do not have to carry plastic bottles along. It strikes me as being a thoughtful facility.

Most workers present in the Goodricke gardens today are second- or third-generation workers. Their comfort levels are high, and they choose to continue what their parents have done, is one explanation offered by most of the managers whom we meet.

Amit Thapa at the Meenglas factory.

Amit Thapa is one such worker, who works at Meenglas. He has been 'since birth' at the garden as his parents worked here too. Thapa works as a gardener and was first posted at the 'big bungalow' but now works in one of the many bungalows that dot the garden. Despite encounters with animals, he and his family have stayed loyal to their space and work. Thapa had one nasty experience when he was walking across to the next village. He was morose and lost in thought, as he was on his way to fetch his wife who had gone to her parents' home after a quarrel with him.

Deep in his thoughts, he did not see the elephant walking right up to him on the narrow path that ran along the boundary of the garden. Quite as if he was a twig lying on its path, the elephant picked Thapa up by its trunk and threw him out of the way. When he realized he had broken his thigh, and the fracture was too nasty to allow him to move away, he started shouting for help, 'Bachao, bachao...' the sharp ears of the elephant picked up the sound and it turned, searching for him in the shrubbery. Luckily, the villagers nearby heard too and rushed to his rescue. 'They called the forest car and took me to hospital.

It took six months in the Siliguri hospital for me to be able to walk again. My brother works here too, he came and took care of me,' he said, adding, 'but I was taken care of by the company all the while.'

Medical help is one of the necessary benefits the gardens offer to their working staff across categories. Often, they try to go beyond what is laid out in the labour laws of the land, building a bridge of trust with the workforce.

'A worker in permanent employment gets full support to live a comfortable life,' J.C. Pande's words are repeated to us at many gardens in many different ways. The worker gets a house for the family and himself within the garden boundaries, ration and medical help, firewood for his cooking needs and schooling for his children. Cycles, umbrellas, shoes and tunics are provided. As such, most needs are met without any spend from a worker's pocket.

This somehow helps wipe away the shock I felt on first hearing the amount most pluckers earn per month. I realize that it is not a cruel bondage as my mind had quickly imagined.

Most families have both husband and wife working in the garden, and as the children reach employable age, often they too join the workforce.

In many gardens, firewood has been replaced by gas cylinders, and that makes their lives easier while saving the environment from smoke and degradation.

PHARMACIST

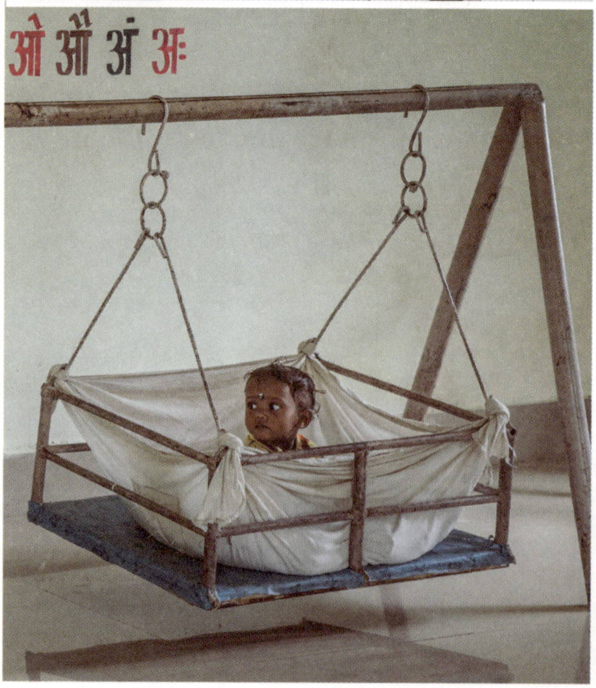
ओ औ अं अः

MEENGLAS T.B. HOSPITAL
याद रखिए

Fighting Nature's Villains

The health of the workers is a prime concern of the group. A healthy worker helps increase production. The fact that diverse gardens have workers hailing from different ethnic groups also necessitates an understanding of their food and lifestyle habits and the effect these may have on their health.

Equally vital is the need to find a medically qualified person who can multitask across medical disciplines, and also find succour in the fact that he lives and practises his knowledge and skills in the isolated confines of a tea garden.

Dr R.R. Banik is one such medical savant, who has made the tea garden his home and adapted to its way of life. Banik operates as medical officer at Meenglas Tea Estate, where he joined after completing his stint as deputy director, health services, Government of West Bengal. Assisted by Senior Welfare Officer, Anirban Sen and three nurses, Banik has managed to change the health profile of the garden.

'Earlier there was a lot of resistance to any kind of medical and preventive health measures,' he said. 'But we worked hard and managed to break down the resistance to inoculation, administer polio drops to the babies and children, and ensure they enjoyed better health.' Dengue and malaria used to be rampant in the villages, but the incidence has come down now with the villagers adapting to the use of mosquito nets, and because of the regular spraying conducted to kill mosquito larvae.

Dr R.R. Banik is the medical officer at Meenglas and has made the tea garden his home.

Banik teaches at OPD camps the importance of washing hands thoroughly before meals, and the 'etiquette of coughing'. It has helped prevent the spread of infectious diseases including tuberculosis.

To fight the prevalence of night blindness in the region, he ensured yellow fruits rich in vitamins were introduced into the local diets.

'We controlled TB through a very concentrated measure,' Banik explained, elaborating that they would visit ten homes on each side of a home with a patient in it, and examine residents for cough or other symptoms for two weeks. The high incidence that showed up was curtailed by such measures, and early identification, treatment and awareness of preventive measures plus incentives by the garden to comply with health measures and family-planning initiatives, made a huge difference.

Meenglas also, like all other Goodricke gardens, has a central crèche where babies are taken care of while their mothers work in the garden. 'We deploy the mothers of babies close to the crèche so they can go and check once or twice a day, or nurse them if necessary,' we are told. Small cloth cradles hold the babies who sleep quietly cocooned in the softness.

At the crèche, we watch, hidden from sight, how eight-year-old Sushila is being taught how to wash her hands to rid it of germs. It is a learning process for us too, who, living in cities, are always in a hurry and do a perfunctory rinse before we sit down to eat.

From 7.00 a.m. to 3.00 p.m., which is concurrent with the timings of the garden workers, the crèche tends, feeds, and trains the children in health measures suitable to their age. Discipline is also taught, and it is amazing to see how quietly and happily the children sit as they are spoken to.

At the Aibheel tea garden, we meet another dedicated medical officer. Dr Omprakash Prasad is now the Chief Medical Officer for the entire group. That implies that apart from his core job of looking after the population of the garden he is stationed at, he is also in charge of all referrals in the group, and decisions on whether to refer them to the hospital at Siliguri or elsewhere.

'The diagnostic facilities here are good,' Dr Prasad said, but added, 'it is a 24x7 job and I am alone here. The ideal strength is at least three, but it is not easy to get people to come, and live and work in such a remote place.'

The garden has, under his control, started free surgical services since 2005 for cleft palate and cleft lip cases, which are common in the region, with the help of two NGOs, Pro Interplast and Howrah South Point. 'We call all the patients and a group of German doctors operate on them at the clinic,' Dr Prasad explained, adding, 'till date 850 surgeries have been successfully conducted, repairing a defect that causes humiliation and health problems for the afflicted.'

The Goodricke hospital at Meenglass, West Bengal.

Surgery is also conducted to address the problem of clubfoot, another health-related issue common here. It could be hereditary and can be identified even on the very day a baby is born, as the foot would be inverted. Early operation as the child turns one, or before it starts walking, ensures quick recovery and complete normalcy.

Regular health camps are also held in the villages beyond the garden, and cases referred to hospital if specialized treatment is found necessary. Eye camps and distribution of free spectacles have helped better productivity, as many pluckers are not aware their eyesight has diminished.

Dr Prasad is now part of the Goodricke family in more ways than his services to the group; his eldest daughter has joined the company and works at the head office in Kolkata.

In 1993-94, the good doctor was also instrumental in establishing a Mother's Club. Twenty women from among workers or dependants were trained in immunization and general health awareness, to take the activities of the medical centre forward.

The Goodricke factory at Meenglas, West Bengal.

A Hero is Born

Thus goes a tale told by Dr Prasad at Aibheel:

'Around 12.30 at night I was called for an emergency. One worker had stabbed another in a fight. The man was bleeding badly and had been carried to the hospital. I was horrified looking at him. He was bathed in blood; his intestines had spilt out and had been hastily and crudely tied with a gamcha. They had placed him on the floor.

'There was no time to lose. With whatever resources I had at hand, my assistant and I managed to operate on him and put his intestines back in place before we sewed him up. It was an emergency measure to prevent him from dying of blood loss or infection. I then referred him to the surgeon at the district hospital 60 km away, for further treatment.

'I was awestruck when he was discharged in four days, with a note that he needed no further work. He recovered completely after convalescence. And believe it or not, I was a hero!'

Heroism had visited the doctor earlier too, though in a less pleasant form. In 1990, while with another tea company based in Assam, Bodo extremists attacked a club during a Diwali party that he was also attending. They opened fire at random and shot down one person. Eleven others were injured, and one among them was Dr Prasad. 'Luckily, the bullet went clean through, and I felt no pain. All those hurt were seniors, so I rushed them and myself to the nearest hospital. Being a doctor there, I had to ensure their treatment first and look after them till they mended. One of them, a lady, was badly hurt; her treatment took three years, and she still limps!'

In the hill gardens, the problems could be somewhat different. Dr Subhash Dutta at the Castleton Gardens tells us about the problems of high altitude compounded by the habits of the workers. Often, unable to afford sugar, the workers add salt into their tea. It was a habit practised in the colder Himalayan regions, which possibly filtered here as a way of flavouring the brew. 'We found many instances of people suffering from high blood pressure,' Dr Dutta says. 'And it often led to cerebral haemorrhage or thrombosis, embolism or myocardial infarction. Besides, they would suffer from spinal or cerebral injuries due to falls caused by dizziness. And in older people, we would diagnose huge internal bleeding. In the plains, it is easy to rush them to a bigger hospital for intensive care; here it is not so easy.'

His clinic can cope with small surgeries, and there is a small dispensary. While simple cases needing attention beyond what the garden clinic can offer are referred to the hospital in Kurseong, the more complicated cases are sent to Siliguri.

Skin complaints centred around the mouth, fungal infestations, bleeding ulcers and psoriasis are other frequent issues the hill doctors have to deal with, arising from poor personal hygiene due to water scarcity and cold weather.

Dr Dutta also sees a growing incidence of lifestyle diseases. Dementia, Alzheimer's disease, diabetes and depression are other problems affecting the workers, all, according to Dutta, 'a new phenomenon due to the changing lifestyle and increased stress of life in the gardens.'

The Goodricke tea gardens of Orangajuli, Assam.

Keeping in Step with Nature

At the Orangajuli tea garden in Assam, pruning is underway. 'Pruning is necessary because, otherwise, the plants will grow too high, and also the process gives plants a new impetus to put out fresh leaves,' Talat Ahmed, who is in charge of the garden and our host, tells us. It is our first stop in Assam, and a series of coincidences has made us feel amazingly at home, over and above the genteel hospitality the gardens are renowned for.

Both Talat and his wife Nishat have friends and relatives whom I know, having spent ten years as a schoolgirl and a junior collegian in Guwahati. We trade stories in the evening, as each common link unfolds to our mutual amazement. The morning after we arrive, the mandatory round in the official vehicle shows us a new side of the tea garden.

'The young plants are pruned the heaviest,' Ahmed explains, 'being young, they will grow faster and soon tower over us as trees. Which is a waste. So they have to be kept in check. The oldest plants are subjected to the lightest pruning, as their growth is also the slowest.'

The cut leaves are allowed to remain around the plant and turn into mulch, providing important nutrients to the root. Nitrogen, phosphorus and potassium, which are vital for root health, are derived not just from the fallen tea leaves but also from the leaves of the shade trees. I see stretches of what must have been rich green expanse now like an undulating sea of brown twigs, stretching

upwards to the sky. There is something pathetic about the sight, but one knows the operation is for the plant's good, and nature will soon dress the twigs in new green.

Further away, in another part of the garden, work is under way to make new beds. Mounds of soft soil are filled into small plastic pouches by workers, who sit in rows. The soil is then beaten tight, so it compacts inside the pouch. The seed is introduced into this and the pouches are covered with hay and water. Nature has to take over now and create the miracle of germination.

Once the shoots are ready, they will be transplanted in rows, into the ground. This process happens once a year, we are told.

Ahmed points to a grouping of tall trees, which, to our surprise, he says are tea trees. If left unchecked, this is how tall they can grow, towering over the

I see stretches of what must have been rich green expanse now like an undulating sea of brown twigs, stretching upwards to the sky. There is something pathetic about the sight, but one knows the operation is for the plant's good, and nature will soon dress the twigs in new green.

garden, their leaves larger and thicker than what the bushes offer, their barks as strong as any eucalyptus. 'We are harvesting some of the trees for seeds, and also some attempts are on for extracting tea-tree oil,' Ahmed said.

While some of the new plants are grown from seeds, others are created by grafting. Twice a year, in autumn and spring, the process of grafting is routinely carried out, to ensure there are enough new plants.

The nurseries where the baby plants are sheltered are a river of green, and the plants with their bright leaves remind me of school boys with spiky, washed hair standing in line for assembly! Verily, life in the tea garden makes one whimsical in thought!

Looking after the older plants and creating succeeding generations of new ones is only one aspect of ensuring a good yield from any garden. The soil, which nourishes the plants, is an equally vital component and needs its share of care.

In every garden we visit on the plains in Assam or in the Dooars, as well in the slopes of Darjeeling, we notice large squares where tall grass grows

Mounds of soft soil are filled into small plastic pouches by workers.

in abundance instead of the tea bushes. This, we learn, is a foreigner that has adapted wonderfully to life in the gardens and plays a vital role in its upkeep.

Originally from South America, Guatemala grass is used widely in tropical countries now to improve and replenish the soil. Often an entire tract of tea bush, which is not yielding enough to make its continued existence viable, is uprooted. The soil, instead of lying fallow, is planted with Guatemala grass, which grows thick and tall and covers the space even as it enriches the soil. In about a couple of years, the grass fixes nitrogen and other nutrients to make the soil ready for tea again.

At that point, the grass is either pulled out and transplanted to another section that needs it, or mulched. It has been proved that the grass mulch improves the yield from three-year-old tea plants by up to 10 per cent.[4]

Once the seed is introduced into the soil, Nature has to take over and create the miracle of germination.

The grass, interestingly, also provides a sanctuary for not just the occasional elephant, but leopards who find it a safe place to have their young, and for rodents who burrow and breed safely in the soil. 'Entering a patch of tall-growing grass can be done only with a lot of caution and preparation,' as one planter put it.

*S. Sandanam, S.G. Jayasooriya and A. Somaratne, 1976. 'Effect of soil reconditioning on organic matter and nutrient status of tea soils and on yield of replanted tea', J. Plant. Crops, 4 (2): 60–67

Some Song and Dance

It's evening time at the Orangajuli tea garden, and there is something afoot. In the patch of green that forms the lawn just beyond the porch, shadowy figures move swiftly about. Noticing the movement from a corner of my eye, I wonder if all is safe. Tea gardens have indeed known cases of real and attempted kidnappings, and though I hold my peace, I wonder for a moment whether we are soon to be given a taste of the wrong kind of excitement.

The excitement is high, but of a very different kind.

A group of beautifully dressed women, anklets and ghungroos tinkling softly, stand in the darkness. Their hands hide shy smiles, and their silver ornaments gleam in the shadowy light.

I realize we are being treated to a dance show.

One after another, the women take their place. They are pluckers mostly, or the wives of pluckers. But here, transformed by their traditional clothes and makeup, their hair gleaming with ornamentation of beads and shells, they are so very different. They dance with confidence, abandon, in their element, with the music of the drums; the male voices energizing them further.

There are three or four performances, each by a different group. Some are soft and romantic, others energetic, but they are entirely captivating. The last group draws us in, locking hands to ensure we keep in step. Now, we are the shy ones, hesitant, unsure of our abilities, till the rhythms takes over. When it ends, flushed and happy, the dancers pose for photos along with the men who look as unlike tea pluckers as can be imagined. It is as if they have shed their everyday garb and gone back to their roots, sure of themselves, with no hierarchy to tie them into corporate protocol or take away their natural expression.

Bishwakarma Kanwar whom we meet the next morning, is justifiably proud of his dancers. A retired garden clerk, Kanwar has been retained to help the staff make the most of his multiple skills: Kanwar is football expert, Taekwondo teacher and dance master all rolled into one.

His Jhumri dance team has won prizes; the many teams trained by him are renowned for being the 'best in Assam'. Proof of which has been evident in the gusto and immersive enthusiasm of the dancers we witnessed the night before.

Kanwar also gets a lifelong pension from the Government of Assam, has performed with his troupes across India as far as Kanyakumari, and featured in a paper in Tezpur University on 'Using Folklore for Community Messaging: Adolescents as Agents for Social Change and Empowerment' (2016). His awards are also on display, including a Kalakriti Samman certificate dated 2017-2018.

Indeed, the yeoman service Kanwar does by teaching young people to dance with pride and grace helps keep their ethnic culture robust and gives them a creative output to channel their energies and competitive spirit into. Besides, it entertains the endless line of dignitaries and visitors who pass through as guests of the gardens of Assam.

A Chain Reaction

Life in the gardens that grow tea has a pace of its own, driven by nature's untiring cycle of growth, rest and renewal. Every single garden employee, be it the plucker, sorter, clerk or boss, is tied to the cycle, and must ensure not a step is missed, if the garden has to deliver the desired output in quality and earnings. Thus, season after season, even as the leaves and buds are plucked off and gathered, they need to be processed immediately for optimum results.

Every garden has its own factory, a place where the sound of machinery at full throttle can be heard continuously, and where the fragrance of tea curls itself into the brain in insidious ways.

The tea that we add to our teapot, be it from Assam or Darjeeling, has gone through a series of processes which, we realize, are ruled by precision and a deft blend of technology and human understanding,

At the Danguajhar garden in the Dooars, we experience our first factory visit.

We don aprons and cover our heads and mouths to avoid any contamination of the precious leaf. Watching how the green, newly plucked leaf bouquets are funnelled in, we are also aware of how different the tea leaf smells when raw. It is a leafy smell, different from other leaves, but different too from the heady smell of tea when it has been brewed. That, we know as a scent that immediately lifts the spirits. This one is cloying and wet.

We look down from the height of the funnels to see the leaves being pushed out on to flat metal beds, after which it will be curled.

This is the withering process, whereby the leaf is dried, and much of its

Bags of tea leaves begin their journey of varied processes at the Danguajhar factory.

moisture is thus removed. Slow fans blow at the trough from either side. While 75 per cent of the moisture is removed from orthodox style leaves from Assam, only 30 per cent is extracted from leaves meant to undergo the CTC (crush, tear and curl) process. Darjeeling leaves have 55 to 60 per cent of the moisture taken out. The higher extraction is to ensure the flavour of the leaf can be maintained.

Once this withering process is completed, the leaves go to the next step. For orthodox Assam teas, the leaf is rolled into a round. But for the CTC, in factories like at Danguajhar, the leaf is crushed and curled. It is a harsh process that breaks through the leaf cell. Rollers cut the leaf, in four stages, as fine as possible. The rollers then roll the leaf to give it the granular shape that every CTC tea drinker is familiar with.

The orthodox leaf faces less punishment and is gently curled on a turntable to ensure the cells are broken through, very slowly and gently.

On the factory floor, the smell of raw tea leaves is different from the familiar heady smell of brewed tea.

The fermentation process is the most technical of the many processes a leaf goes through. Fermentation ensures the oxidization of the leaf. This is when the green leaf loses its original colour, as oxygen turns it darker. The leaves now go through the CFH or Continuous Fermenting Machine, a belt from below which tubes send up fresh, moist air. The tricky bit here is that each set of leaves have their own timing, and there is no knowing at which point of the time-curve the process could get complete. Alertness, and a strong nose that can discern that the leaf is ready, is the only way of ensuring the process does not leave the leaves underdone or overdone. If too early, the tea will taste green and raw; if too late, the tea will be harsh and unpalatable. By now, the greenish tea has become coppery. The thumb rule is that fermentation takes about an hour and a half for CTC, and up to two for orthodox.

The drying process is the last one and is done to arrest the fermentation. The leaf is subjected to a high temperature of about 130 degrees Celsius for about 25 minutes. To ensure the leaves do not have more than 3 per cent moisture, a coal-heated furnace sends hot air into the drier cylinders. The result: dry tea leaf, that comes out warm to the touch.

The entire output is now sorted through round-stacked machines of different sizes. As the leaves pass through them, they pick out fibre and other unwanted additions that might yet remain, the chutes send the bigger granules through a main funnel, while smaller grains are pushed out of the side vents. The tea leaf is thus automatically sized and can be priced accordingly. 'In all, we are told there are six sizes: BOP/ BOPSM / BP / OF /PD /DUST.'

Mounds of tea to be weighed, packed and priced accordingly.

A Lesson in History

In the Amgoorie tea garden, visitors can experience a sense of history if they go to see the factory. This is where CTC tea was made for the very first time.

Amgoorie is one of the oldest Assam gardens. Established in 1865, it spans 976 hectares, which also makes it one of the largest. Three divisions, Tiru, Tiphook and Amgoorie, make up the gardens, which stretches almost to the border of neighbouring Nagaland.

A ride across the gardens takes us through different terrains, much of it plain, some of it undulating and then a bit of it across a stretch of water and up a slope. The tea here has special status too. 'It's the best,' Paran Das, manager of the gardens and our host, says with obvious pride. And indeed buyers come from far and wide to place orders, and the tea goes out to supply boutique tea brands like Wagh Bakri and Society Tea, besides finding space at Starbucks. The Starbucks teas are packaged to state the grade, period and quantity of the leaf, though some blending may also be part of the package.

Also popular in the UK, tea from this estate is bought by Taylors of Harrogate and by another famous UK company, Bewleys. Das tells us that his garden tea finds special place at Harrods in London too.

Amgoorie is thus the top earner in Assam for CTC and owes it renown worldwide for the quality of leaf. Of course, the credit goes as much to nature which provides the unique combination of terrain and soil that adds its bit to the colonial profile of the bushes.

It was at Amgoorie that, in 1931, Col Sir James Buckingham, a planter,

established the first CTC machine. 'Till then, leaves were either sold as orthodox or rolled by hand,' we are told as we take a round of the factory. Experiments with machine rolling resulted in the now universally recognized CTC system of processing tea leaves. 'In fact, CTC machines are exported from India,' Das adds.

The CTC process has indeed become universally popular. All the Dooars gardens now specialize in CTC, and in Assam too, besides Amgoorie, Borbam, which is close to it, and other gardens, have adopted the process. The gardens of Cachar all process tea through the CTC method.

Amgoorie is one of the oldest and largest Assam gardens.

The Taste of Tea

Of course, with all the fragrance of tea in its many stages, the brain is by now clamouring for a taste. So we join the group that is testing the samples, as they go through a quality check.

Like wine tasting, tea tasting is a fine art. It requires a sensitive palate; a tongue that is not addled by rich spices; and a strong, sensitive nose. Also, an understanding of colour in its aspects of clarity, depth and brightness. The tea tasting follows strict rules that may differ with gardens and the tea being brewed. So, here, five grams of tea leaf are boiled, and covered for 5 minutes to create an infusion. The product is placed on top of the lid; the infusion is in the cup.

The leaf is examined to see if it is black. Leaf of a uniform colour shows it is from a similar kind of plantation, while grading in colour indicates a blend. Tasters also look for buds, which add to the quality of the tea.

The tasting of the liquor is done in a special way. Tasters use a spoon or drink directly from the cup. They slurp the liquor in so that it is taken in with plenty of oxygen that passes over the inside of the mouth, including the palate and tongue, to ensure an even taste. Tasters also check if the tea is mellow or sharp in taste, brackish or smooth. Tasting is done without milk, and also with milk added. The aftertaste of the tea is also noted, as it can range from pleasant to arid.

After slurping the liquor in, the tasters spit it out.

The appearance of the tea is also marked. A bright appearance of the infusion indicates the keeping quality of the tea. Even when milk is added, the tea must look bright.

Tea tasting with Paran Das (extreme right), manager of the Amgoorie gardens.

The verdict of the tea tasters decides the price and grading of the tea for the market.

We decide to taste some of the tea liquors too. I cannot bring myself to slurp, or spit, but I am able to discern different flavours and strengths as I sip from one cup and another. Perhaps, if I learn to slurp and spit, there is a lucrative career waiting for me! Especially since I seem to quite like life in the tea gardens.

Vikas Gajmer, manager at the Castleton tea estates.

But there is a simple truth in the fact that most tea-garden managers who succeed at being happy at their job are those who have a kinship with nature and are able to entertain themselves by being in her company.

Just Another Way of Life

Atul Asthana, MD of Goodricke, has an interesting story to tell about his career graph. Interesting because it is like a template that most executive lives in the gardens seem to be following.

Since he jumped from his first job at Escorts within six months of joining it, to join Goodricke, Asthana has been a tea-garden man.

'I saw an ad in the paper asking for engineers for a tea company soon after I joined Escorts, and it intrigued me. We had a sudden holiday spell following the assassination of Indira Gandhi, so I decided to present myself for the interview in Calcutta. It was simple as even the travel was being underwritten by the tea group.'

Asthana's memories of his interview with the then HR manager of Goodricke, Ajay Jain, make him smile. 'He brainwashed me, and I was ready to jump. For one, it sounded interesting and different and, of course, the better salary was a draw. My father, however, was doubtful. He was an engineer too, working with SAIL, and was not sure it was a good idea, but he was open-minded enough to say, try it out.'

He took sick leave from Escorts, to 'try it out' and joined Chulsa garden in Dooars, thinking to himself he would give it a try for three months and go back if it did not work out. But he did not return. 'There was no hierarchy in the gardens then,' he remembers, 'and I was soon looking after the factory, In two and a half years, in 1987, he was posted to Assam at Orangajuli, and remembers

Atul Asthana, MD.

with pride that it was a 'prestige posting' as the Assam gardens, then only two in number, were considered the company's 'gold mines'.

It was like being thrown in at the deep end, but Asthana learnt everything about tea gardens as the factory's assistant manager. It was a turbulent time, with trouble brewing in the state, but he was cocooned in the garden, and 'it was a good social life, with a good club and all comforts'. His learning included handling different types of manufacturing: three types of orthodox teas, different varieties of CTC teas, to suit Indian and UK markets, and it led him into 'a quick learning phase about the different types of manufacturing'. It was not long before he was handed the duties of a garden manager too.

But life in the Assam gardens was not all smooth then. As a tea planter in charge of a number of young executives as well as a sizeable labour force, his responsibilities were manifold. When the first kidnapping took place, of a manager from Nonaipara garden, who was whisked away by militants, the group

The tea gardens in Nonaipara run adjacent to the boundary line of a thick forest area.

realized that security was not tight enough and had to be stepped up.

'The militants picked him up from his bungalow and vanished with him, then sent a ransom note,' he recounts. Of course the company promptly paid the money demanded. 'Actually,' he adds, 'neither the militants nor the company knew what to do, so they both went through the expected motions. Within 48 hours, the manager was returned.'

Of course, the incident resulted in all the ladies being evacuated, and all the men shifted into the main bungalow amidst a subdued state of fear that the kidnapping drama may happen again. Bow-and-arrow guards were put on duty at the gate as an emergency measure. 'Luckily for them and us, no militants with guns turned up again,' Asthana says laughing.

According to him, Assam is the basic learning ground for all manager aspirants. By 1991, two more companies with six estates came under the

Goodricke umbrella in Assam, and there was enough variety of work to make it a perfect training ground

Pranjal Neog, currently HR head with the group, emphasizes that Asthana's mode of entry into the group as a fresher just out of college is still quite the norm at Goodricke. 'Ninety-five per cent of the time, we hire at entry level,' he says, 'and recruit trainee assistant managers from agriculture or engineering backgrounds. The plantations need these skill sets. Regular students from the humanities field also qualify for recruitment. Interviews are conducted by a panel made up of the operations head, HR manager, head of engineering and quality control and the senior manager, operations. The short-listed candidates are sent to the MD for the final interview before the list is finalized.

'Most recruits are around 24–25 years of age, and all we ask is that they have the curiosity and desire to learn and grow. At Goodricke, they can plan a career for the next twenty-five years.' The company keeps a reserve of recruits, and when the reserve starts depleting, hires afresh.

Neog agrees that there are challenges in the recruitment and retaining of executives. 'Relocating a young graduate from a city where he has his family, his circle of friends, his regular addas and hang-out joints to a far-off garden where his company will be limited to a small circle, is a risk we take, for no one knows if the person will adjust, or give up.' To ensure life in the garden remains attractive, executives are encouraged to develop and nurture hobbies, take up sports... We give them a clip of life in the garden, so they do not find a surprise

Happy tea garden managers have a kinship with nature. J.C. Pande, senior manager, Danguajhar, examines the quality of the tea leaf.

waiting there,' he adds. 'It is quite like an IAS officer's first posting, only in the garden, the recruit has no magisterial powers.'

Postings of the fresh recruits follow a plan that depends on manpower requirements. 'Sometimes there is a strong risk of attrition, at which point we try to meet the person halfway, counsel him, or post him out to what could be a garden more suited to his needs.' Neog says attrition can happen even with recruits who come with garden experience, as one culture can be different from another, and the group then has to go the extra mile and be forthcoming enough to integrate such people.

Gardening is a hobby that most young recruits are encouraged to adopt. Nature is their friend and guide in their job through the years ahead, and gardening is one way to get to understand nature's ways better. Recruits are also encouraged to develop understanding and empathy, as they have to manage different groups of workers across a variety of situations. But there is a simple truth in the fact that most tea-garden managers who succeed at being happy at their job are those who have a kinship with nature and are able to entertain themselves by being in her company.

Asthana must have gone through it too, but the system is much more regulated now, as the group has many more gardens in its care. The initial training is rigorous through the first year, with a foundation course that includes study, writing of papers and developing people skills. New specialized fields call out to the recruits to better understand irrigation, pruning, plucking, and reports on these are required to be submitted to HR. If adequate, the recruit could be rewarded with an upgrade, if not, he submits to further training and advice. After a monthly report is evaluated through the year, the recruit could be made permanent and considered ready for an upgrade.

'Perhaps the reason we have so many seniors who started with the company fresh from college is that the group goes way beyond terms of employment to help an employee,' Asthana says. 'Managers go beyond the call of duty. To give one example, there was an employee whose daughter was diagnosed with leukaemia. The company gave him all the help it could, to get her treated. Today, she is well and a student in college,' he says.

Asthana's trajectory to MD is not very different from that of most officers of the company. They move from garden to garden, with growing responsibilities, and the company tracks not just the profits they bring in, but their problem-solving quotient, their people and inter-personal skills as well as the variety of skill sets they acquire along the way.

Marriage is a big milestone for managerial cadre employees in the garden. Recruits are not allowed to marry for three years, so they can acclimatize to the demands of life in a garden. However, finding a partner and setting up a household that includes a spouse with no experience of life in the garden can pose new problems.

'I was lucky,' Asthana says. By 1994, he was posted in Harmutty in Assam as manager and a married man. He remembers that he got two days, leave to effect the change in his marital status. In two years, he was on to his second stint in Nonaipara, was inducted into Operations by end of that year and moved to Siliguri by 2000. He was by now in charge of Operations in six gardens, including two in Darjeeling.

'In determining the quality of a batch of tea, fifty marks go to the leaf and fifty to the factory,' he explains, talking about the most important lesson learnt along the way. 'If the field gives 49 per cent, the tea should be good, unless the factory messes it up.'

Typically, senior managers move into the main office. They could take up responsibility in the different departments, or continue to oversee gardens as visiting agents, like Lalit Sinha does.

Asthana remembers his own move up to becoming vice-president in 2013 of the entire Assam group of gardens. There was another VP in charge of the Dooars. He does not say it, but there must have been a healthy competition to see which of them would beat the other at being best at his job.

'I would tour fifteen days a month,' he recollects. 'It was exciting but exacting; the biggest challenge was to lift the region to the category of a diamond mine. With wages going up, I had to up the quality to ensure that the sale price was higher than the cost of manufacturing the tea.'

'Times are tough for the industry,' Asthana admits, 'but Goodricke is keeping ahead of the crisis. Thanks mainly to the fact that we follow best practices and have loyal and dedicated employees at all levels.'

From the Plains to the Mountains

Tea is tea, but Darjeeling tea is different. Or so the world believes. And indeed, anyone who has enjoyed a cup of the golden liquor of Darjeeling will vouch for the unique flavour and lightness that the combination of mountain air and the soil of the region impart to the drink. Thus, it is the only tea in the world to wear the geographical indicator (GI) tag and is valued for its subtle, unique flavour the world over. In fact, Darjeeling tea was the first Indian food product to win the GI tag, as early as in 1999, when the Act first came into existence.

Just to recap a bit of history I picked up along the way, the tea gardens of Darjeeling date back to the 1830s, to the time when the East India Company set up a hill station here. In 1839, Dr A. Campbell, who was the district's first superintendent, sought the blessings of Governor-General Bentinck and planted the gardens, using seeds of tea plants smuggled in from China. Though he could not have been aware of how natural factors in the region would magically work on the output that would be derived from the leaves, he realized that the sun and natural drainage in the region could ensure a good yield.

Darjeeling decides to give us a thunderous welcome. It pours all the way up the winding roads, with flashes of lightning lighting up the dark masses of hillsides. But our driver is experienced, and soon we are at the Thurbo Tea Garden. As if finding itself thwarted by the fact that we have continued bravely on, the rain ceases suddenly, leaving only a searing cold behind.

The warm welcome we get from the Rais, whose wooden house is quaint and cosy, more than makes up for the cold outside. Rai gives us a brief history

Thurbo in Darjeeling greets with bursts of sunshine in between spells of rain.

Gaily coloured homes of the Darjeeling plantation workers.

of the gardens and plans the morning's itinerary. It will, of course, include a garden visit during which we could, if luck favours us, get our first view of the iconic Kanchenjunga.

In the morning, the peak cannot be seen, but the newly washed slopes of tea are poetically beautiful. We drive down past the gaily painted homes of the workers. Each house has flowers growing in pots, and sprouts a TV antenna, and reflects housekeeping skills that speak of house-proud inhabitants. Motorbikes lean against some gates, and Rai informs us that many workers prefer to ride a taxi rather than walk to their place of work. It is obvious that the Darjeeling gardens are the five-star among tea gardens, and its workers are automatically privileged.

Beyond this workforce that forms the bulk of permanent pluckers, a sizeable number of villagers from the surrounding Mirik village are happily and gainfully connected to the garden. Rai puts the number at around 12,000.

J.D. Rai. Group Advisor and General Manager, Thurbo.

Verily enough, as we tour the gardens over the next few days, we realize each garden here is a brand unto itself, proud of its history and its place as a supplier of the coveted teas. Thurbo, for one, holds the distinction of being the first garden where tea was planted in the 1930s. Fringed by the mountain on one side and the Mirk Lake on another with two rivers flowing through, Thurbo's wonderful vistas are also home to wildlife species like porcupine and wild boar, deer and, of course, the leopard. Once a year, the garden becomes a tourist spot, when the cherry trees burst into bloom, filling the sky with pink blossom that scent the air. We are either too early, or the blossoms are delayed by rain, so we miss the sight. Bees love Thurbo, and the local honey is prized only second to the tea.

Though each garden has a history and a leaf unique to itself, Margaret's Hope is one garden that seems to have earned a special place as a brand. Google the name of the garden and thousands of websites pop up about it! Also renowned in the history of the Goodricke gardens in Darjeeling is the name Castleton, for the fact of it fetching what could be the highest price that tea has ever earned, with 110 kg being sold at Rs 13,000 a kg in 1992! 'It was during my tenure in Castleton,' Rai says; 'it was a world record at the time'.

The story he narrates has us imagining the scene of the auction, and the fine tea being bid for and bought by no less a client than the emissaries of the emperor of Japan. He prized the tea he had bought greatly, and with an emperor's benevolence and style, had bone China sachets made, in which he distributed the tea among his closest friends and officials. In fact, at the Castleton Tea Garden, visitors can see the entry made by the emperor's buyer, Yumi Nakasugawa, in 1992. The book's earliest entry dates to 1990.

Perhaps the mantra that Rai has spread among the staff and workers under his care, in his extended duties as a visiting agent and general manager of the Goodricke gardens in Darjeeling, is what makes these gardens so special. 'I tell my people, work satisfaction is the best reward, and it shows in the fact that our produce sells instantly,' Rai says.

His memory of the gardens goes back a long way. When he joined the gardens, things were very different. For one, the mail was not delivered by a postman. 'There was a dak wallah, and he would also do all the shopping for the big houses in the gardens. The memsahibs would make a list of the things they needed and give it to him every time he went to get the dak. He would go in the morning and come back by evening with the purchases and the mail. Those days, the manager would have an Ambassador car, and the assistant would have a second-hand jeep. It was all very primitive by today's standards.' The advent of television changed everything. 'In 1985, we could get reception from Bangladesh on our TV sets, which otherwise would reluctantly let us watch snatches of Doordarshan punctuated by long periods of wavy lines and flickering screens. Bangladesh would entertain us for 5 to 6 hours every evening. Then, in 1995, a TV tower came up here and life changed for the better.'

Rai, who grew up in the region, has been in the gardens of Darjeeling from his first job thirty-four years ago, and to him, Darjeeling tea is a 'total passion'. He avers that only those who totally love nature can spend a life in the tea

Of all the Goodricke Gardens in Darjeeling, Castleton is renowned for fetching what could be the highest price that tea has ever earned.

gardens, but it is an immersive and very fulfilling life for those who adapt to it.

The leaf creates a spell that is very powerful, the deep satisfaction of harvesting and manufacturing a new batch of the world's most coveted leaves can be heady and overwhelming to a young man responsible for some of the processes. 'Sometimes,' he adds a bit wryly, 'the passion of the executives towards their job can be a real problem for young brides spending their first years here.'

Rai says the success of Goodricke in Darjeeling has been the passion of its employees for the job. 'Those who work for money fail miserably,' he intones.

Over the years, the tea of the region has grown in status to gain worldwide renown. Rai has, in his tenure, seen buyers who came to buy 100 or 200 kg of leaf, now investing in tonnes.

There are eighty-seven tea gardens in Darjeeling, covering a total of 19,000 hectares. The Goodricke gardens in Darjeeling contribute about 10 per cent of the total tea from the region, but all of it is highly prized.

Nature dictates a slightly different regimen here. Thanks to the cold weather, the gardens are never above 6,000 feet from sea level, as frost would kill the plants or damage the leaves. The first flush appears by late March, pulling the workers into the gardens in the cold mornings to start plucking. Despite its lightness of flavour, the first-flush picking could command Rs 5,000 to Rs 6,000 a kg, though 'there is no upper limit'.

Post noon, we take another chance at sighting the Kanchenjunga, but to no avail. And adding to our disappointment is the fact that we have just missed the blooming of the cherry blossoms, which turn the hillsides a radiant pink!

MARGARET'S HOPE

Partnership
ETP

Legendary Gardens

The Darjeeling gardens are different from one another, and each has its own legends. The terrain changes too, with slopes often steep and forbidding except for the locals who, born and bred in the mountains, are sure-footed and unafraid.

A long drive to the other side of the valley takes us through mist and rain to Castleton Tea Estate, which by now has piqued our curiosity enough. It is as if we are expecting to see bushes tipped with leaves of gold.

But the gardens there have posed their own challenges to the company, before yielding their booty. The soil and the climate at Castleton have conspired to create a leaf that is particular to the gardens here. According to records, the bushes here were replanted in 1985, after Goodricke took over two separate adjoining gardens, Castleton and Springside, a year earlier.

'Most of the garden was of the original China bushes,' according to Vikas Gajmer who occupies the manager's bungalow, which has a story of its own. The bushes yielded a premium brand of tea, but they were old, and the yield was poor. The entire garden had to be uprooted and replanted, a slow and arduous process, done manually, bush by bush. More tension was added by the fact that the bushes took a long time to establish themselves.

Planters check roots to see how strong and healthy they are. If the root system is good, then, even if the yield is lower than ideal, they let the plant continue, and rejuvenate it. However, if the roots are facing the possibility of decay, the plants are uprooted and used for firewood.

The Castleton plants offer up leaves with muscatel, and a flavour that is 'not

The soil and climate at Castleton have conspired to create a leaf that is special to the gardens here.

Yellow tea is much like green tea, but with an additional step to seal the yellow colour.

prevalent elsewhere'. Gajmer explains that muscatel is a spicy, musky, fruity flavour that makes the leaf aromatic. It is the result of some sap-sucking insects that could partly damage young tea leaves, especially in the months when the second flush is ready. In a bid to protect themselves, the tea plants produce terpene, which works as an insect repellent. The pests are repelled, and the terpene adds a musky flavour, which is unique and highly prized by tea aficionados.

And indeed, it is evident why. At a blind tea-tasting at the factory, the thumbs up is for one particular brew, which Gajmer says, with a triumphant smile, is the muscatel.

At Margaret's Hope, Samir Gupta tells us the story of his experiments with the Darjeeling tea plant.

'I wanted to grow yellow tea,' Gupta says, 'and tried many experiments to do so.' Of course, there was much trial and error, across gardens, but finally at

Margaret's Hope, in 2019, he was able to make his efforts bear the kind of leaf he wanted. 'I started initial studies and research during my stay at Thurbo, with active participation by Suman Das and Vikas Chhetri. When I was transferred to Margaret's Hope, I persisted and continued with my experiments. My colleagues Anup Khondo, R.K. Rai and, especially, Vikas Singh helped immensely. And luckily, this time I got the result I wanted.'

We stand on the edge of his garden overlooking the valley, a view the bungalow is famous for, as he pours out a light-yellow liquid into the glass cup. Indeed it is neither brown nor golden, but a pale yellow. The colour gives the tea its name.

Obviously, yellow tea is much like green tea, but with an additional step which 'seals the yellow' colour. Under this process, the tea polyphenols (catechins) are first oxidized to attain the yellow tinge, and then further processes help preserve the colour and aroma of the leaves.

We taste the tea, and it is stronger than the colour leads us to expect. Gupta watches us closely and is happy when we smile. For him, it is vindication that taste and colour are both pleasant.

Reading up on yellow tea, I learn that it has many benefits. Fat burning and increased metabolism are two of them. Step aside green tea... there is competition waiting around the corner!

Moonlight Sonata

Nature helps create moonlight drama in Darjeeling, at a ritual that is as exotic as it is rare. In the garden that is adjacent to Castleton, moonlight tea has become a tourist attraction. Gajmer says his garden, too, can offer moonlight tea, and indeed it is one of the teas we taste at the factory. But while Castleton prides itself on its muscatel varieties, Makaibari, one of the region's oldest tea estates, has made a ceremony out of moonlight plucking.

At Makaibari, the moon plays nature's agent along with the soil and water. Following a calendar that reads the alignment of planets, the garden plans the plucking of leaves on particular full moon nights during the plucking seasons that begin in March and continue till October.

It happens during the first flush, when the water level is low in the plants, that plucking by moonlight is carried out. Perhaps it is part of the tourist show that makes it the way it is, skilled hands from among the garden pluckers come dressed in ceremonial costumes accompanied by the beating of drums and blazing torch lights that should not just light the way but also keep wildlife away, pluck the leaves by the light of the full moon. The plucking starts around 8.00 p.m. and ends by midnight so that processing can be done much before dawn, as the leaves need to be protected from sunlight and heat.

The uniqueness of the plucking as well as the ceremonial trappings have added a certain mystique to moonlight tea, pushing its price even higher than would have been expected, if it had not been given such publicity.

A Unique Process for a Unique Tea

Of course, the process of making the leaf of the Darjeeling tea plants yield their liquor is mighty different from the processes followed in the plains. The most important difference is the focus on minimal handling of the delicate leaves.

The tea plant in the mountains of Darjeeling yields smaller leaves than the plants of Assam, which have larger, broader leaves.

Tea factories have a unique fragrance, a blending of green leaf with the aroma of roasted leaves. In Darjeeling, the fragrance acquires a mellow sweetness, as if fruit essences have mingled into the air.

Walking through the Castleton estate factory, we learn about the precious and guarded process surrounding the extraction of Darjeeling tea. Leaves from the gardens are brought into the factory twice a day. Once at 1.00 p.m. and again at 4.00 p.m. The process of withering here is a slow, long-drawn-out one, so as not to break the leaf, and can take up to 16 or 18 hours and stretch across a whole night.

The leaves are withered in batches on different machines, as each machine has a certain capacity. Moreover, each type of leaf is treated separately, using hot air to draw out about two-thirds of the moisture or being left to dry naturally, depending on flush and the type of tea required. Each batch of withered leaf is about 90 kg. These are now rolled, and a twist given to the leaf so that the cells are ruptured and the liquor extracted. The machines turn at 42 rpm. Timing is of importance here. First-flush leaves are exposed to 15 minutes of rolling; others get 25 to 30 minutes of the treatment.

The Castleton tea factory.

This is followed by a process of sorting, where the leaves are passed through sifters to sort the unrolled leaves for a second round of treatment. Gajmer stops by every machine to personally check the processes and the leaves as he takes us through. The workers, in turn, stop to respond to his questions if any. Visitors to the factories are not infrequent, so we do not command much attention.

Fermentation of the leaf here, too, is a vitally important process and needs to be carried on with the utmost care. The leaf is spread gently by hand on steel beds. On closer look, it proves to be moist, semi-crushed. In Darjeeling, the fermentation process is about leaving the leaves to be exposed to ambient oxidization forces. Each batch is separated and marked by the 'Ghani' (local term for the slip, on which details are entered). The drying time is checked before the leaves are lifted. Once the time written on the board is met (we read 1 hour 40 minutes), the leaves can be lifted and collected in a vessel, or gamma, and care is taken to not overload the vessel lest the leaves at the bottom get crushed.

The fermentation bed is immediately cleaned for the next lot. The leaves have emerged from their process more capable of imparting a richer colour and aroma to their brew.

Even as the oxidation process is nearing completion, the driers are being prepared to receive the leaves. They are kept ready 10–15 minutes before the fermented leaves are lifted.

Driers have set inlet temperatures when the leaves are introduced into the drier, depending on the pick of leaves. The oxidized leaves are not fed into the drier. The entire tray must be filled, uniformly. Again, the 'Ghani' is used to separate batches of leaves and ensure there is no mixing. Each Ghani may have a different inlet temperature, and the workers have to check and reset accordingly. It is skill and caution, and diligence, at work here.

We watch workers collecting the dried leaves and letting them cool, before weighing them. Once it is done, the leaves are taken to the sorter room, and kept in different batches as indicated by their respective Ghanis.

'This leaf is ready to make the best tea you could want,' Gajmer tells us. 'But the factory work processes are not over, and the leaf cannot be sold till it is sorted and graded.'

By now, we are looking at a dry, dark version of the fresh green leaf that we saw at the start of our factory tour. The grassy smell has also metamorphosed into a rich aroma, which makes us think it indeed must be tea time by now.

But Gajmer has more to tell us. The leaves travel by conveyor, like royalty being transported to the final stage of their long journey. Here, the lower grades will be separated from the richer, higher grades.

Once more, the leaves pass through a shuddering drive-like contraption. The leafier selections are sent out on top, the dust filters through the bottom. The larger leaves are promptly sent right back for yet another round of shaking and sifting. As the hierarchy suggests, what gets sorted at the top is pick of the

Sorting

lot, while the dust is the lowest in the chain and will sell the cheapest. Most of the dust goes into making the tea bags that, thanks to fancy packaging, sell at fancy prices.

A fine cloud seems to have enveloped us. Gajmer tells us it is the dust rising from the sorting, and fluff. This is officially the 'waste' and disposing it is another 'official' process that the garden must undertake with responsibility. Vacuum machines run on the corridors to pull away the dust permeating the air.

Explaining the various machines, Gajmer points out they are all top of the line and dedicated to high performance. He shows us how the Britannia Sorter or Garden Sorter easily segregates all grades of leaf. We take in the scent of the premium grades, flecked with the white of buds, and are shown samples of the other grades, from primary to broken, to powdery and dust; the last best used for boiled tea.

Though they pluck the moonlight leaves as a routine part of their plucking schedules, the quality is special with pubescence present, and such leaves have fetched a price of up to Rs 21,000 a kg!

Stalks are removed at the final stage, a caution in case there are many leaves with a lot of stalk. The sieve works in layers, holes send the leaf through, while the stalk is channelled into the bin. 'It is a Chinese machine,' Gajmer says, and we wonder why the labour-rich country created a machine to replace work that could keep many hands busy and employed. For international use, I suppose.

The machine is also fitted with small magnets at all stages, to remove impurities, and this is the last stage for the leaf before it is safely packed away. The newly tiled floor is a matter of pride for the factory; it replaced the older wooden floor that had developed cracks and would attract mildew.

The factory, too, bends to the dictates of nature.

Gajmer points out the small roller cabinet kept for the occasions when nature decides to send out speciality tea leaves or a small picking. 'When Castleton picks moonlight tea leaves, we do not want them sorted as they are full leaves, so we run them through this small roller cabinet,' he explains. 'Also, at the beginning of the season, when the pick is between 10–15 kilos, we do not want to waste time waiting for a larger consignment and run the leaves through this.'

Though they pluck the moonlight leaves as a routine part of their plucking schedules, the quality is special with pubescence present, and such leaves have fetched a price of up to Rs 21,000 a kg!

All Darjeeling leaf must be brewed, as boiling will turn the tea too bitter to relish. The magic way is to use 140 ml for a cupful of tea, boil it without over boiling, and brew the leaf for 5 minutes.

And Now a Tale for a Rainy Evening

Right through the day we spend at Samir Ranjan Gupta's bungalow at the Margaret's Hope garden, he has been carrying along a folder. 'It's a collection of notes that you can use for reference,' he says, and I thank him, adding that I am taking copious notes of my own all the same. Yet, when I ask him to hand over the sheaf to me, so I can stash it away in my room, he says he will hand it to me when we are leaving. Perhaps, there may be points to be added...

The garden is beautiful as is the bungalow, and my room is large and spacious with three doors. One leads in from the living room, where we spend the evening chatting. The other to the bathroom. And a third door, opens into a room that is a kind of study, as the desk and chair proclaim.

'That is our sun room,' Gupta explains, 'we spend our mornings here in winter because the glass lets the sunlight in and the room is really cosy then. I also work at the desk in the winter days when work in the garden is not as demanding. And tomorrow, you will have your breakfast here,' he adds. Sounds like a cute plan.

The three doors for some reason disorient me. I often find myself opening the study door when trying to enter the living room. Then correct my mistake. It is a bit of a joke. Then I realize it is because the room is shaped a bit oddly, with more corners than normal, to allow the sun from many sides, during different times of the day. The architecture of each house we have visited is uniquely suited to the place and its climate.

We tour the house and its grounds, taking in the swing, which I enjoy a quick

The manager's bungalow at Margaret's Hope.

ride on, the tennis court and the large dining hall with its array of artefacts.

Finally, over dinner, I manage to wrest the folder from Gupta. For me, moving from garden to garden, any recorded help is invaluable, and I do not want to forget taking along this backgrounder my host has so thoughtfully prepared. Perhaps, I tell myself, I will also read it through at night and jot down salient points into my own notebook.

But we chat late into the night, and by the time I reach my room, I am ready to drop. I fall asleep, overcome by the stupor that an excess of good food brings along, to wake up a couple of hours later, realizing I have to brush my teeth and take my vitamins. That done, I stop momentarily to look at the patterns of moonlight, and then I am back in my bed to quickly fall asleep again.

The next morning, the sun smiles down as the household help sets a small table in the sunroom and we enjoy breakfast. As we are leaving, Gupta reminds me to take along the folder. I assure him I have packed it. He gives me a long look, then asks, 'Did you read it?' 'I wanted to,' I say, 'but I fell asleep. I usually read all the material I gather in the day once before sleeping, but yesterday, I missed.'

To my surprise, he smiles and says, 'Thank God. I wanted to warn you not to read it. Because it has the story of the ghost of Margaret's Hope.'

Tell me, I say, and I listen to the story of how Bara-Ringtone Tea Garden was renamed Margaret's Hope.

The story goes back to the early twentieth century, when the garden was managed by an Englishman, Cruikshank. His daughter, Margaret, loved the place, and took great pleasure in the house and its sunlit room. When the time came for her to go back to England, she promised that she would return. But that was not to be. The young girl died during the voyage, and her dream remained unfulfilled. The grieving father changed the name of the house and the garden in her memory, to Margaret's Hope.

'The story goes,' Gupta says, 'and I have mentioned it in the note in the folder, that Margaret's ghost wanders through the house quite frequently. They say she comes in from the west side main guest room, goes to the study and walks to the tennis court through the veranda outside. That is why I was holding on to the folder, you see?' he adds.

It dawns on me then that the room Margaret occupied is the room I was sleeping in, and her favourite room was the study just a door away. 'Maybe it was not one of her visiting days, or maybe I slept too soundly,' I say, as we pile into the car to drive away. Later, it strikes me, chilling my heart for a brief moment: What if it had been her moving through my room that awakened me! What if I had opened the study door instead of the bathroom door? What would I have seen? It was her favourite room after all!

Margaret's Hope, deep in the hills of Darjeeling, has the most romantic name.

The Photograph That Was Never Taken

The quintessential picture of a tea plucker is of a gaily dressed woman, standing waist-deep among the tea bushes, a basket suspended from her head hanging behind her to receive the leaves she holds in her hands, as she smiles into camera. It is a pretty accurate picture. Tea plucking is more suited to women's softer, smaller and more nimble hands, and one has only to watch the speed with which they pluck to know that part of it is instinct and the rest pure practice.

Many of the pluckers we met seemed intrinsically happy souls, and though they did not sing in high-pitched voices as Hindi films would have us believe tribal and rural women do as they go about their chores, they seemed quite capable of doing so. The only time I saw a set of surly women pluckers was one cold but sunny morning at Badamtam in Darjeeling, when a few had been rounded up to pose for photos.

The reasons for their surliness were partly justified. The agitation for bonus had just been launched, and though the Goodricke gardens were offering an amount close to the demands of their workers, the other gardens had held out a much lower percentage. Knowing that the issue would not be resolved till a consensus was achieved among the many gardens, which would not be before the impending Diwali festival, must have been demoralizing. Worse still was the fact that on what was considered a day off, the women were rounded up by a supervisor for a photo shoot.

Of course, everything went wrong for us that morning. For one, the women were dressed in their party clothes, looking like a fancy-dress group. And if they were out of sorts at being dragged out, they turned decidedly surly when the supervisor, hoping to impress, ordered them to pose this way and that. We had come for natural photographs of the pluckers; instead, we were getting a line of stiff, unsmiling women standing in an unnatural cluster. And then the sun, which had set out to shine on the shoot, suddenly decided to get surly too, and disappeared into the mist that literally came out of nowhere. Of course, there was no photograph worth retaining!

A Garden without Women Is like a Plant without Buds

Besides adding colour to the gardens with their clothes and their chatter, the women of the tea gardens are also one of the reasons the gardens manage to retain their labour. Shaibal Dutt admits that the migration of workers to other job opportunities is high. Rail and road construction are among the biggest reasons that tea-garden labour moves out. The hospitality industry at the lowest levels draws them to the cities.

But the women realize soon enough that in those jobs their men only drink away the cash after a hard day's work, and there is no benefit to the family. Also, the lack of social security is in sharp contrast to the cocooning that garden labour enjoys. Thus, even if the men choose to move out seeking other jobs, the women prefer to stay behind and continue in the garden. As Dutt puts it, 'The women are the backbone of the garden; they are the ones who keep the gardens running'.

To ensure that the women who are not directly employed by the garden or those who live as dependents of male employees, find ways to improve the family's financial status, the company has started teaching them other skills. By involving women in collaborations that the garden does with buyers, where they speak to Starbucks managers in their own language; and teaching them skills in sustainable living, Goodricke has helped more women become contributing partners. 'They are taught to repair and maintain solar devices, to train in women-

Goodricke has helped more women become contributing partners.

centric hygiene management roles and safe midwifery, and learn bee-keeping. It keeps them gainfully occupied. And they help set up an internal revenue model inside the gardens, and get empowered too, in the bargain.'

Asthana, the MD, adds his tribute to the women of the gardens. But his thumbs-up is towards the wives of managerial staff. 'It is not easy for a city girl to leave behind her surroundings with its hustle and bustle and tuck herself away in the middle of nowhere,' he says. He is right. As Kalpana Lajmi's film *Ek Pal* showed, life for an educated, socially active, extrovert can be a very tough adjustment when she moves into a garden bungalow. Her husband is busy, as the garden work is practically morning to evening, with work starting just before daybreak. Even beyond the actual running of the garden are the preoccupations with labour issues, health and social problems among them, which might affect productivity – all of which alienates her further from companionship. 'Garden wives will either adjust and become the true support of their husband, or walk

Many wives can boast of nurturing show-worthy gardens. Seen here is the manager's bungalow at Badamtam.

out of the marriage,' a senior official opines, adding, 'luckily we see more of the former in our experience, over the years.'

Wives who get involved in the nuances of garden life get busy and stay happy, I am told. They interact with the garden population, which is in its own way a microcosm of the world outside. Others find they can use the opportunity life has thrown them to develop skill sets, like embroidery, painting, and writing. Van Gogh is a favourite source of inspiration, and at Badamtam as well as elsewhere, we saw versions of the impressionist's sunflowers recreated by the lady of the manor. 'I try my hand at painting, it is both soothing and fulfilling,' Nandita Sen said, as we gazed at her rendition of Van Gogh's work, and a few other paint-and-brush creations. Gardening is particularly rewarding, and without actually getting their hands dirty, many wives can boast of nurturing show-worthy gardens that could make it on the cover of *House & Garden* magazine. 'The gardens are yet to bloom in full,' J.P. Bajar, manager of the Meenglas Tea Estate, says when we exclaim over the profusion of colours that is spread out on the lawns outside the house. 'Once spring comes, you will see the real spread.'

As much to encourage the hobby as to give its results exposure, Goodricke holds an annual flower show, just before its annual sports show, in late January, every year. All through the year, garden wives work with malis to ensure they can present the best blooms and compete for the coveted prizes.

'We try our best as a company to ensure wives find a level of comfort,' Asthana says. One example of that is the story of Nigel D'Souza's wife, Soma. A highly accomplished executive, she did not want to give up her job with IBM when she moved into the garden. Luckily, IBM allowed her to work long distance, and she moved into the garden carrying high-speed data in her laptop. Having his wife by his side happily engaged in her own career, was a huge support, and helped Nigel grow, according to Asthana.

Wives do sometimes have a problem pursuing their own careers, according to Sangita Krishan who served us a sumptuous lunch before we took off on a round of the Lakhipara garden searching for the elephant herd. Sangita is a school counsellor and has sometimes found it frustrating to follow her career without breaks, as every change in her husband's posting necessitates a new place of work for her. 'But I manage,' she says smiling, 'and then there is always so much to do.'

Meenu, Gajmer's wife, on the other hand, pursues her career in beauty and fashion in Siliguri, and shuttles between Castleton and Siliguri. 'I come here whenever we have guests, and to ensure the house is running smoothly,' she says.

Dolly Das at Amgoorie agrees. 'I think besides being a support to all the young wives on the estate, a manager's wife also has a fulltime job maintaining his house and home. Guests are frequent and come not just from across India, but from other Camellia properties in Kenya and the UK; then buyers drop in from across the world, and we need to ensure the staff is trained enough to cater to both their housekeeping and food standards.'

Actually, as Nishat Ahmed told us during our visit to Orangajuli, workers often refer to the manager of a garden as 'Mai Baap', but it is the Mai who has a role that reaches into the lives of the many who form the population of any garden.

Often, a senior wife will take a junior executive's bride under her wing, teaching her the unwritten norms of life in the tea gardens. 'In due course of time, her husband will rise in the hierarchy, and she needs to be prepared to take on the additional duties and responsibilities that will be her share,' Dolly Das explains.

While most senior managers have children who are either studying elsewhere or are grown up enough to hold jobs of their own, Gupta's wife, Barnali, still

Flowers bloom in the garden at Margaret's Hope, Darjeeling.

has their young son to groom and take care of. It is for her a double duty, as the guests are frequent at Margaret's Hope garden, famous for its beauty as well as for its tea, and because her son has special needs. However, thanks to the fact that, as part of its CSR, Goodricke runs a special school in Siliguri, her son gets the help required in schooling and training in many aspects of normal living. His going to day school thrice a week has made 'a huge, positive difference', and helped Barnali juggle between being a helpmate to her husband, a competent hostess and a caring mother to her son.

In fact, the MD has words of praise for all wives. 'They are essential supports, and vital for the physical as well as mental well-being of their spouses,' he says. He explains that a tea manager's job, at any level, is a taxing one. 'So a wife ensures he eats good food on time; it is never the same if the menu is left to the cook in a bungalow. We see the difference when a wife goes home for a wedding or takes a holiday from her duties.' Also, with so many different levels of person-to-person issues, she is the one disinterested person who can help her husband arrive at fair and unbiased decisions. Managers tend to get stressed, as they have no avenues for advice or help to take decisions on thorny issues; that is when a wife proves invaluable. Besides, her mere presence is often a stress buster.

And, of course, when it comes to alerting the women in the garden about issues like feminine health and the risks of being fooled by predators trafficking in women and girls, the manager's wife plays a role that is effective, as she is seen as a mother figure by the workers.

Actually, as Nishat Ahmed told us during our visit to Orangajuli, workers often refer to the manager of a garden as 'Mai Baap', but it is the Mai who has a role that reaches into the lives of the many who form the population of any garden.

Stretching Out to Help Those in Need

Interlink, in Kolkata, is a strong vindication of Asthana's statement that the company rests heavily on the contribution that the employees' wives bring in to the group. Started in 1984 by the Late Savita Bhasin, wife of a former MD, Interlink evolved from an idea to an institution that helps special children once they cross the age of sixteen. The idea she conceived was to help differently abled children and adults to use their time creatively or in the company of others and get some kind of vocational training in the process. Once a differently abled child reaches the age of sixteen, they have to discontinue special schooling, and is suddenly left to his own devices. Interlink would try and support the teenager, taking on the baton of responsibility to guide him into adulthood.

Started under the guidance of the Late Gina Levete, who had an Interlink Centre in the UK, the initial activity was about bringing those in need of special help in touch with artists, who could teach them to use colour and create forms to express themselves. Initially lacking a space to accommodate those who sought their help, Interlink helpers would send them to various institutions. Dancers, artists and painters were taken on the Interlink payroll and asked to interact with the attendees in the spaces given by these institutions as part of the outreach programme envisioned by Levete, who visited India several times between 1987 and 1997. Even today, the social worker-cum-dancer's vision of 'creating a network and connecting individual artists from different disciplines to create opportunities through visual and performing arts for people with disabilities and the socially disadvantaged', remains the blueprint the centre follows.

Now, having a building of their own located in Elgin Chambers, the main hall the Centre uses can support thirty to thirty-five attendees at a time. Not all those enrolled attend every day, but whoever does come gets complete attention to help them further their expressiveness and communication skills. 'My wife, Bandita, is currently in charge of Interlink,' Asthana says, adding that the mantle automatically falls on the MD's wife. 'She is completely involved in the project and works closely with the hands-on staff to ensure it runs effectively and smoothly.' Bandita oversees the running and administration of the centre, visiting it regularly two or three times a week.

At the centre, we meet teachers and volunteers. Passionate about the task they have taken up, they are vocal about the headway the centre has been making, slowly but steadily, considering the fact that their wards are of varying ages and different needs and abilities.

Anuradha Dutt, wife of Shaibal Dutt, senior manager, operations, calls Interlink her 'second home'. But naturally, she is also keeper of the keys to the place and is one of the first to arrive at the institution, and the zeal shines through her eyes. Explaining the process of helping the wards who seek Interlink, she says the first step is to separate the child or teenager from the mother, who is naturally overprotective. Their love often stunts the child's capacity for independence and self-expression, so it is a vital first step.

When the children first come to the centre, especially the teenagers, teachers say they are slow and restless. They show no interest in doing anything. It takes a lot of effort to get them to interact first with the teacher who is given their charge, and then with others. Sometimes the process is long-drawn and calls for infinite patience on the part of the teachers; other times, the sun shines through and a ward shows great progress and promise.

One such is Kaushik Banerjee who, in 2018, was awarded the National Award in Dance for being a Role Model among Persons with Disabilities. The student of Interlink had trained in classical dance and was chosen for the award because of his ability to connect with the audience, which proved he had crossed the line into being able to connect with the outside world. 'It was a proud moment for us at Interlink when he, accompanied by his mother, received the award from

Yoga instructor Chandan Sarkar, who specialises in holistic yoga training, conducts a class at Interlink.

the Vice-President of India, M. Venkaiah Naidu at Delhi's Vigyan Bhavan on 3 December 2018,' Dutt says.

Dilip Kumar Mondal is student Anupam Mondal's father. He meets us in the office room, accompanying Anupam, who is celebrating his birthday on the day of our visit. It has been a year since Anupam has been coming to the centre, and his father is happy with the progress his son is showing. 'I see positive change,' he says, 'he used to be restless; now he is much more settled, quiet.' Anupam's IQ is about 25-26 and he does need help. 'We could not afford any other place, so when we heard of this one, I brought him here.'

Skills taught at Interlink aim to draw out students from their shells and make them feel joy in the creative process and rejoice in the result of their handiwork. So they learn to stitch aprons, to embroider and paint on fabrics. Examining the cushion covers and towels embellished by the students tells us that each of them has discovered his or her potential to a great extent. In fact, some of the work is worthy of a professional artist or embroiderer.

Interlink also takes a stall at the Annual Sports Day held by Goodricke at the Dooars. 'This year we sold a substantial amount of creations by the students,'

Skills taught at Interlink aim to draw out students from their shells and make them feel the joy in the creative process.

Dutt says. The money earned is used to help the needy among parents and students.

Susmita Roy, who also works at Interlink, is in charge of the centre's outreach programmes. She decides on the artists' schedules. Starting as a secretary to the director, her zeal ensured she moved on to take responsibility of reaching out with help to schools and to the bastis (nearby settlements). Recruiting normal children, she oversees the spread of awareness about special needs of the disabled and other such educational themes as they train to perform skits at street corners. Earlier, the skits have also been performed for jail inmates, but the practice has since been discontinued.

Interlink continues to add new projects to expand its scope. In 2019, it added Founder's Day celebrations to mark the birth anniversary of the Late Savita Bhasin. Sit-and-draw competitions, annual picnics, and dance and drama performances by students of other schools are part of the activities through the year. 'It keeps our wards interested and is a welcome break from routine,' according to Roy.

And when Niloy Banerjee received the National Award for his feat of long-distance running on World Disabled Day 2019 and shared a cup of tea with President Ram Nath Kovind at the Rashtrapati Bhawan, the selfless teachers at Interlink felt their hearts swelling with joy.

Students also participate in a holistic yoga class every Tuesday, with the practice created on the lines of what two teachers, Chandan Sarkar and Madhumita Banerjee, learnt at a specialized holistic yoga training and certification course. The teachers had been sponsored by Interlink to attend the course from a Bangalore-based instructor. The Tuesday classes are very effective and much liked. The Interlink teachers always try to keep their activities as close to a normal school as possible. They organize celebrations for Holi, Raksha Bandhan, Christmas and other festivals. Rabindra Jayanti Day is marked by song and dance, and teachers get special acknowledgement on Teacher's Day. As Dutt says, 'Our calendar is full, and we keep the teachers and students fully occupied.'

Dilip Kumar Mondal is student Anupam Mondal's father. He meets us in the office room, accompanying Anupam, who is celebrating his birthday on the day of our visit. It has been a year since Anupam has been coming to the centre, and his father is happy with the progress his son is showing. 'I see positive change,' he says, 'he used to be restless; now he is much more settled, quiet.' Anupam's IQ is about 25-26, and he does need help. 'We could not afford any other place, so when we heard of this one, I brought him here.'

The first milestone he says his son reached was that he started taking off his own shoes. 'In the beginning, he would not do it even when we repeatedly told him to. His mother would have to take them off for him. Then, at the centre, they took him into the room, and away from us, and said, you have to do it yourself. And he did it. When he took off his shoes, everybody clapped, and he was happy. He responded. His mother is not allowed in the room as she keeps trying to hold him,' Mondal senior says.

Anupam offers us a slice of cake. He accepts our congratulations, the shyness is obvious and communication limited, but as Dutt points out, it is a huge step forward, and he is now communicating with his teachers, and she is his favourite. Anyone working with a severely introvert personality will understand how big a milestone it is for him to interact even in a limited way with complete strangers.

The teachers at the centre are also in praise of the progress shown by yet another student, Niloy Banerjee. He is one of the older boys, born in 1982. Teachers say that the thirty-seven-year-old now runs marathons, and trains for it by getting up at 4.00 a.m. to run for 2 hours. 'In 2014, he ran 5 km; in 2016 he doubled it. And this time he ran 21 km,' Dutt says with obvious pride.

And when Niloy Banerjee received the National Award for his feat of long-distance running on World Disabled Day 2019 and shared a cup of tea with President Ram Nath Kovind at the Rashtrapati Bhawan, the selfless teachers at Interlink felt their hearts swelling with joy.

Ready in an Instant

Subir Ganguly's life in the Aibheel tea garden beats to a different rhythm. As manager of the instant tea factory that Goodricke runs since 1996, his work concerns machines that look like shining robots from a sci-fi film.

As we walk around the gleaming, tall steel machines that dominate the factory hall, making the few men working on them seem diminutive, Ganguly tells us that 'the instant tea process starts where the black tea process ends'.

At the factory, the leaves go through an entirely different process: they start by decanting the liquid to separate it from the slurry of the spent leaves by means of a machine called the 'Decanter'. Evaporation is then the next step, followed by a clarifying process to remove insolubles.

Once the leaf goes through these processes, a final evaporation is required to dry it up to 45 per cent. At every stage, some drying takes place, but once the final evaporation is over, spray drying ensures the process is complete.

According to Ganguly, instant tea is a 'sleeping giant' in these times of ready mixes and instant everything. The huge convenience factor has already made it popular not just in the UK and the US, but also in Japan, which has a long traditional link with tea and the ceremonial way of drinking it. It is catching on in India too, with some companies offering instant tea in flavours, for the harried executive living far away from home.

Goodricke sells the tea powder in bulk, and companies like Wagh Bakri convert what they buy into 3-in-1 mixes, with milk powder and sugar added.

Ganguly has been with the factory only for the past six out of the twenty-eight years he has served the company, but his passion for his job is quite obvious. What excites him as much as the processes he has explained is the R&D that the factory is constantly involved in. The experiments involve quality improvement, control and improving environmental sustainability.

As we sip from cups of flavoured instant tea in Ganguly's spotless cabin, where his degree in Agricultural Engineering is proudly hung, he acknowledges that the engineers of the plant truly share his passion for the job. Three main parameters, which are considered to be of prime importance as far as instant tea is concerned, include colour, clarity and taste. The factory maintains a close vigil on these parameters and might just be one of the reasons behind its rapidly growing popularity in countries such as Holland, the US, the UK, Germany, Taiwan, Japan, Singapore and Australia.

Strict quality control is a must to ensure no bacteria or contamination has smuggled itself into the powder at any stage. Sampling of the end product to check this is done with cultures, and with nature giving of its wisdom, and sunlight.

In fact, sunlight is one of the primary arms nature holds out for this enterprise. One hundred and thirteen solar panels on the factory roof help create the hot water required through the many processes. 'Sixty-two per cent of our requirement for heating water to 80 degrees comes from the sun, conventional methods are used for the remaining percentage,' we are told. Also this cost-saving process allows only minimal steam to escape, and thus maintains the temperature in the machines with less energy input.

Savings at every step is necessary as the cost of the raw material is higher. Darjeeling and Oolong tea leaf is preferred. And 4 g of mix is required for one cup of instant tea, as against 3 to 4 g of regular leaf. Ganguly explains that there are two types of instant tea which they produce: (1) Hot water soluble (HWS) and (2) Cold water soluble (CWS). While HWS dissolves at 80 degrees Celsius, the CWS can dissolve in temperatures as low as 10 degrees Celsius. The cold-water mixes can also double up for a warm drink, though the reverse is not feasible. Depending on the raw material used, which includes the likes of BMF (broken mixed fannings), Black tea, Green tea, Oolong tea, Darjeeling tea, the plant produces a varied range of products in their instant form, namely, Instant Black Tea, Instant Oolong Tea, Instant Green Tea and Instant Darjeeling Tea. The factory produces 350 metric tonnes of instant tea in a year.

The plant is certified by FSSC, Kosher, Halal and RA (Rainforest Alliance). So Tel Aviv is aware that the tea is certified Kosher, and UAE knows it is Halal. Rain-forest certification isn't a certificate that is prominently displayed. The leaves come from across gardens, catering to the orders placed by the factory with the Calcutta office.

He further, enthusiastically, goes on to explain how the plant engages in developing various customized products by utilizing its 'Pilot plant', which is a miniature of the main plant, where constant trials are taken up to develop new products to match customers' requirements.

Ganguly's pride in the project under his charge shines through as he talks of

the plant's effort in furthering the man–nature partnership. A constant effort is on to harness the solar or green energy and conserve water. A total of 212 CPC (Compound Parabolic Concentrator) panels on the plant rooftop harness the solar energy during daytime to heat up the water to 80 degrees Celsius, thus meeting 60–70 per cent of the heating requirements through these solar panels. This is a vital step in saving energy and reducing carbon emission. The Government of India, Ministry of Non-renewable Energy, awarded Goodricke for this commendable project. Taking the effort of conservation one step further, the plant recycles the water that is generated at different stages of evaporation, thus saving almost 50–60 kl water per day.

As we sip from cups of flavoured instant tea in Ganguly's spotless cabin, where his degree in Agricultural Engineering is proudly hung, he acknowledges that the engineers of the plant truly share his passion for the job. Three main parameters, which are considered to be of prime importance as far as instant tea is concerned, include colour, clarity and taste. The factory maintains a close vigil on these parameters and it might just be one of the reasons behind its rapidly growing popularity in countries like Holland, the US, the UK, Germany, Taiwan, Japan, Singapore and Australia.

Though there are four other players in the field, Nestle's, Tata, Hindustan Unilever and Ahimsa Chemical, (A.V. Thomas in Cochin produces instant green tea). almost all of the Goodricke produce is exported.

Thinking Beyond Tea

A seed that was planted to fulfil a small need is now a shade tree providing nourishment and shelter to a huge community.

The Goodricke School for Special Education in Siliguri, in the twenty-seven years since its inception in 1993, has built a reputation as a CSR initiative that has a soul and countless helping hands. Anita Chaudhuri, wife of a senior officer with Goodricke and parent of a differently abled son, who had training in special education, started the school in a small way, hoping to help other parents who had children with special needs and realizing that most would not know how to cope.

In a report published by the Goodricke School for Special Education, Chaudhuri details the hurdles in the way of her mission.

'In the initial years, no one was ready to rent us a house when they came to know it was going to be used to impart special education. With great difficulty, we found a small place to start our work.' Thus the school began, housed in a small building that had been taken on rent. Today, the institution boasts of a large, sprawling building that has classrooms, workspaces as well as a canteen, dining room and play areas.

The building itself is symbolic of the thought that has gone into the establishment of a facility to help a section of the child population that is largely ignored. Built in three phases, it followed the vision of Canadian architect Anca Hangnau, who was coincidentally visiting the area. Working with Mohan Sharma, her colleague, Anca drew up a blueprint for a building that put the

MEET OUR ARTISTS

PPB

children's needs in the forefront, ensuring their comfort and easy acceptance of what would be an alien space, far removed from the familiarity of their homes. Funded by Goodricke, the building took shape as small, related clusters linked by wide and airy corridors.

Throughout its construction, Gordon Fox, chairman of Camellia Plc, of which Goodricke tea company is a part, made repeated visits, ensuring that any hiccups in the progress of the work would be eased away. The first phase was finally ready in 2006, and the students and teachers celebrated with a song and dance programme attended by both Hangnau and Fox.

By 2010, more classrooms and a large auditorium with a well-appointed stage

was added. Assembly sessions and dramatic and cultural activities were assigned to this space.

Realizing that the students needed skill developments according to their individual capabilities, the third phase included a computer unit even as more therapy rooms were added. A hydrotherapy room was part of the final plan, as well as facilities for in-house training.

Nothing symbolizes the spirit of the school as clearly as its head, Dr Susama Nayak. Under her care are approximately 200 students, many of them from the Dooars area and some from further away. Sixteen teachers and four resource teachers add to the small army that Nayak heads in her movement to assimilate

Dr Susama Nayak.

special children into their households and into society.

'I literally grew up here,' Dr Nayak says adding that her father was a renowned doctor attached to a nursing home, who, after his return from acquiring his medical degrees in London, had worked briefly with Goodricke. Her own destiny had her befriending Anita Chaudhuri, while they 'were studying for a post graduate diploma in teaching children with multiple disabilities (the course has now been renamed as BEd in Special Education) together.'

Fired by her own vocation to help special children, Nayak rounded up her learning with a doctorate in allied psychology, thus equipping herself to address social as well as mental needs of special children. Though her path first led her to work with NGOs in Delhi, including at the well-known Amar Jyoti Rehabilitation Centre where she served as a lecturer, she finally started working with her fellow-student Chaudhuri at the modest facility she had set up. Nayak moved up to be the principal and continues to hold the reins of the school's operations.

She wants us to take a round of the school building. She talks animatedly about the work the school is doing. 'Parents, teachers, helping staff are all part of the team to help the child, I am the face and the voice, but the real work goes on at many levels. It is a tough fight against nature having held back while blessing a child, and a slow battle to help a child emerge from his disability, but we fight on.'

The wide corridors we walk along are bright with posters and happy, positive quotes. Many have been created by the students. Low ramps with railings, and easy to open doors speak of thoughtfulness, and we are told that the bathrooms are also specially modified to make use easy for the most challenged child. The classrooms we peek into are large and airy, and safe. Every aspect of a child's needs and the problems they might encounter in normal spaces has been envisaged and managed.

Nayak explains that the school can manage a maximum of 200 children, though 'not at the same time'. There is a roster of 180 students on board; they come for day care, often with their parents, sometimes without, and spend the day with the teachers and care givers, learning skills that they can carry forward and perfect at home.

Students from a range of disabilities are admitted, including the mentally challenged and those suffering from autism spectrum disorder (ASD) and cerebral palsy. 'Sometimes the children suffer from more than one condition and that makes it very difficult. It needs patience and skill to reach our children,' Nayak avers.

Children are grouped in classrooms according to their cognitive skills and age, so that each class has an integrated set of students with multiple disabilities. Activities could include those 'related to physiotherapy, hydrotherapy, speech

therapy, multi-sensory and occupational therapy and vocational skills'. Besides these, there are classes for computer training, and vocational training for students, who are ready to take the next step towards integration.

Nayak explains that the first step is to help the parent understand his or her role in the teaching process, 'because the child has to spend more time at home and their progress can only happen with parental help. The school only deals with day scholars, boarding brings too high a responsibility to undertake. The parents have to accept; acceptance is the first step to treatment and social integration. When we get a child with multiple disabilities, it is like staring at many zeros. Acceptance is the 1 before the zeros. Acceptance anchors the child with the parent.' Though it is true that each parent deals with the fact of a disabled child differently, it is a harsh reality that must pass through denial and questioning stages to understanding and acceptance. The school, we are told, helps hugely in this.

Severely afflicted students are sent straight to the special learning section, where the first step is to teach them self-care. 'Children learn to brush their teeth, straighten their hair; it is a slow, step-by-step effort to even reach the point where they learn to put on their clothes and button them, or slip on their shoes.'

We watch an 'advanced class' where a group of older children are being taught housekeeping tasks. Laying the table, washing, drying. Simple tasks that one does while singing a snatch of a film song are laboriously carried out, one slow step at a time. But it gets done, and as important as the tasks themselves is the coordination between those doing the different tasks, the passing of the plate, or spoons. 'The family must coax the child to continue these tasks at home,' Nayak says.

While the school works with a student till the age of eighteen, a child of any age below can gain admission. In fact, the youngest child at the school was admitted at 18 months of age. A child is referred to the suitable class immediately on admission and gets into the intervention programme. Term assessments track progress and steer the child to move as close to mainstream as his or her abilities will allow. 'Achievements are measured against the individual educational plan, which benchmarks the student's potential. Reading, writing, drawing, self-care are some of the parameters here. Depending on the level of mental growth and improvement at each assessment, a student moves up the many levels, from therapy and playgroup to the vocation unit.'

'Each student has a need not addressed by mainstream education,' Nayak explains. Parents, too, are encouraged to join group programmes in the school and learn to cope with behavioural issues of their wards.

Activities in the school range from baking to sewing, painting, yoga, sports, music and exhibitions where other schools could participate and interact. Tea packing is a process that students who can manage the task graduate to, and it is heartening to see tea leaves being carefully filled into large bags, which are weighed, the details noted, and the bags packed shut. It feels as if the Goodricke mission reaches full circle here.

The success of many of these activities is indeed evident. We are treated to biscuits baked by the students, and they are indeed delicious, worthy of being packaged and sold in the open market, if the scale can be ramped up. The buntings that have been put up to mark the fact that the school is in its twenty-fifth year are also the students' handiwork. And as we leave, the paper bags we are handed have been created by the children.

Many of their students have started working in sheltered environments such as workshops. The more enterprising run their own business.

'Each child is unique, and we never have a dull moment here,' Nayak sums up. 'These are pure souls, and we only do our best to help them to the utmost.'

Debashree's Story

(as told by Dr K.N. Sharma, father)

'My daughter, Debashree, is six years old. She was about two and a half, when we noticed that her development milestones were delayed. Her cognitive and social interactions were quite lower than normal. As a doctor and radiologist, I realized time was of the essence.

'The developmental paediatrician we approached referred us to a child psychologist, who in turn suggested therapy be started immediately. Thus we came to the Goodricke special school, as it was the nearest, and had a reputation for being amongst the best. Debashree has been coming here close to three years now, for three to four days a month. The rest of the process continues at home.

'Thanks to the early intervention, there has been progress, where there may have been none. Her speech is clearer, though not quite normal; she speaks random words, and is yet to get systematic in sentence composition. But her toilet training has improved.

'My wife is an engineer and works for the government. But outside work aside, we have to give Debashree a lot of attention and care. As parents, we have a vital role. Often, we learn by watching her and try and understand her. At times, she leads us by the hand and shows us what she wants or does it herself. Though there is a tendency to drop things.

'The restlessness in her and the continued hand movements have been controlled, she is able to sit quietly now. She goes to playschool, where she has to interact with normal children. Usually, she has been avoiding loud sounds and sitting by herself, but in the last three years, that has been changing slowly.

'We try and continue at home the tasks that the school teaches her. It takes a lot out of us as parents, especially after a full day at work. Patience is something that helps immensely, but we had to learn it as we went along. After all, everyone knows, "nobody can teach a child, like its parent can".

'A big milestone was when she was able to express affection; it filled our hearts. She tries now to mingle with her younger brother, the child is just two months old, but he seems to evoke a response.

'For us, each day is a new day, a new learning. And I have to tell myself at times, this is not something that will get resolved in a hurry, and that I must hold on to my patience.'

Swarnavo Gupta's Story

(as told by Ravindra Prasad Gupta, father)

'My son had his first seizure when he was two years and seven months old. It was a horrifying experience for us to watch. I remember the date clearly: 18 September 2010.

'We took him to Vellore to treat the seizures. The medication dose they gave him was obviously too high, though we did not know it then. Instead of 8 ml, the dose was at 15 ml. By this time, he was reduced in weight to 9 kg. He started losing his ability to walk. We took him to NIMHANS in Bangalore, but there was no bed available in the near future, so we went to Apollo Hospital in Chennai.

'The treatment for seizure, steroids, had an adverse effect. He started losing all his functions slowly. He would dribble saliva continuously, and by now I had to carry him. I was worried he would die.

'We stopped the steroids, stopped the medicine on the basis of a second opinion. But by then, my son had stopped eating. He just would not accept food. We had to hold him down, hold his hands, his head and force-feed him. He was too thin and his body had no reserves. Food and nourishment were necessary,

'Finally, we decided to come to Siliguri. My wife is a nurse; she had maintained a complete file of all the treatments he had undergone. We carried it with us when we met the doctors here.

'The medication for seizures was stopped, and treatment for the underlying cause was started. Epilepsy is an associated problem we were told, and as parents we were encouraged to work with doctors to help the school identify the kind of seizure he suffered.

'He was put into therapy and on vitamins. By now he was as thin as a finger, almost. A terrible sight that shook us to the core. We continued to force feed him. But the school said, "Do not do so, he will grow a stronger resistance to food. Let him feel hungry."

'It took a lot of inner strength on our part. He took very long to feel hungry, and we, his parents were eating our regular meals through the day. But it worked, though it was really painful for us. But now, he is taking food to his mouth willingly.

'He has gained weight, is about 40 kg; though that is still thin, but he is definitely no longer in the danger zone.

'Till he came here, he had no control over his bowels, now he goes to the toilet, cleans himself if I give him a mug. He has learnt to put on his clothes, though he has yet to learn to put the buttons on.

'I am in the tea leaf business. But for my son, I have sacrificed my work time. I go once a week now. I have put him with a caretaker but am always on standby.

'I have handed my business to my nephew and elder brother. He is also hearing-impaired, who has learnt how to cope. And as president of the Association of the Hearing-impaired, he tours all over India.

'I know my son will also improve slowly. Edge closer to normal. But how much, only time and effort will tell.'

Nina's Story

(Nina shares the role a parent plays in extending the initiatives the school begins to help a special child.)

'Ananya is ten. When she was two, she was still crawling. When she started walking, she also grew aggressive, and mostly against herself. She would hit herself repeatedly. It was obvious something was wrong. We took her to Delhi, and there the doctors diagnosed ASD.

'Ananya has been coming here to this school for the last two years, three times a week. She used to come by bus, and I would come too, whenever the teachers called me. When I come, they tell me what they do here to help my child and show me how I can continue it at home.

'I have to teach her self-care, life skills that most children learn automatically as they grow. Ananya has learnt to fold clothes, lay the table; she does mopping, dusting. It uses up her energy. She tends to be hyperactive, jumps around and that has to be channelled into actions with more meaning.

'Her mind has also developed enough to recognize brand logos; now she can place them in the slots with pictures to match.

'We need to work very hard on communication with her, and it is challenging to keep her in class. Her growth pattern is erratic, and there is no way we can classify it or put her into a stereotype of developmental activities or treatment.

'The fact that her visual perception is strong was noticed early, and teachers are using it to improve her attention span. We are now trying word matching – her name, my name, her father's name. For her, words are pictures, she does not yet see them as letters. But it is a start. And we cannot but go one step at a time; we cannot skip steps, or she won't progress.

'A bridge is what parents provide, understanding a child's needs. We as parents have to unlearn a lot and listen to what the child wants.

‘I was in government service in Kohima. But I have shifted here and given up my job since. It has meant handling her alone at home, but it was a necessary decision for her sake.

‘We as parents must go as far as the child goes. That is the only way.’

Homes

Badamtam

Amgoorie

Thurbo

Meenglas

The Tea Room Kolkata

Margret's Deck

About the Author

Sathya Saran is best known for her long association with *Femina*, which she edited for twelve years. She is also the author of a diverse variety of books. *The Dark Side* reflects her love of the short story, while the critically acclaimed biographies, *Ten Years with Guru Dutt Abrar Alvi's Journey*; *Sun Mere Bandhu Re: The Musical World of SD Burman*; and *Baat Niklegi toh Phir: The Life and Music of Jagjit Singh* bear testimony to her love of cinema and music. Sathya's latest book is a biography of Pt Hariprasad Chaurasia.

Currently Consulting Editor with Penguin Random House India, Sathya also teaches fashion journalism at NIFT Mumbai, Kangra and Srinagar.